HEIAN

First Edition

Published in the United States by Hudson Hills Press LLC, 74-2 Union Street, Manchester, Vermont 05254, USA.

Distributed in the United States, its territories and possessions, and Canada by National Book Network, Inc. Distributed in the United Kingdom, Eire, and Europe by Windsor Books International.

Exclusive representation in Asia by EM International.

Founding Publisher: Paul Anbinder

Executive Directors: Randall Perkins and Leslie van Breen

Manuscript Editor: Margot Page

Art Director: Seiju Toda

Photography: Masaya Suga

Designer: Eiji Takada

Manufactured in Japan by Nissha Printing Co., Ltd.

Library of Congress Cataloguing-in-Publication Data on file

ISBN 1-55595-237-2

HEIAN

COMPOSITIONS BY SEIJU TODA

INTRODUCTION BY VICKI GOLDBERG

Hudson Hills Press

New York and Manchester

Quiet Life

VICKI GOLDBERG

This is, obviously enough, a book of photographs, but Seiju Toda is not a photographer. This particular distinction does not rest on the old question of status that preoccupied the likes of Man Ray, who took photographs but did not want to be knocked off the pedestal of art onto the lowly ground of photography. Photography has come up in the world since Man Ray's day; the term "photographer" no longer consigns an artist to the confines of technicians and craftsmen, and artists who have only limited photographic skills openly use photographs in all their enterprises. Toda, a leading art director and graphic designer in Japan, has been recognized as a prominent artist since he was in high school and has had more than twenty one-man art exhibitions in his own country and the U.S. These exhibitions cut across media, including photography.

Since the mid-1970s, he has been using the medium to make works of art that play with the kinds of issues that preoccupy contemporary artists, such as the human eye's imperfect recognition of reality, the ways we experience different reproductive media or different modes of performance, the process of making art, the very nature of art, the representation of motion, and the nature of light.

In the series called "Heian," he worked more like a movie director with an entirely compliant cinematographer than like a bona fide photographer. Toda neither focused the lens nor clicked the shutter but meticulously, painstakingly, instructed a professional who could provide him with the technical means of accomplishing the exact image he had in mind. In contemporary art, the long and paradoxical history of photography in the service of art—from the beginning it was expected to be "a handmaid of art"—has joined the equally long and paradoxical history of photography's recognition as an art in itself. This union has produced countless photographic works of art that are no more (and no less) essentially about photography than 1960's factory-made sculpture was about factories.

In the 1960s, photography sidestepped onto the gallery scene. Sometimes it stood in for art made in other media, especially when art began to court impermanence as a virtue, an idea that became almost a cause in that decade. The camera was not merely a useful tool but virtually the only way certain artists had to document (and exhibit) ephemeral events or works of art.

Many of these artists were looking for ways to expand art's horizons and circumvent museums by taking their work outside the usual exhibition sites or making it so transitory that museums could scarcely house it. Photography was called in to document site art like Robert Smithson's or Dennis Oppenheim's, or performance, including such temporary art as Jean Tinguel's eccentric piano that ended its performance with a real crescendo, exploding and destroying itself in the garden of the Museum of Modern Art. Some of the artists who were staging protests against the gallery and museum system ended up showing photographs of their work in galleries and museums, so that photographs sneaked into the world of art through the back door.

The use of photographs as records or stand-ins for works of art that were either made in some sense to be photographed or could not be exhibited except in photographs announced a movement that has gathered force ever since. The notion of constructing scenes to photograph took fire in the 1970s and later in the work of people like Laurie Simmons, Ellen Brooks, Sandy Skoglund, James Casebere, and Thomas Demand. In the 1980s it became popular among Japanese photographers.

Seiju Toda brings his own sensibility to this tradition. He has been interested in the ephemeral since the mid-1960s when he was a sophomore in high school and began his artistic career with a performance. Marbles covered with fluorescent paint were dropped into transparent tubes from offstage left and right; they rolled through the tubes, glowing in a darkened theater, and dropped into a Japanese wooden washtub on one side and a metal bucket on the other, producing a sound environment as well as a visual one.

The performance was a tribute to John Cage, whose

work had been introduced to Toda by a high school teacher, and who so inspired the young student that he determined to become an artist. Launching his career with a performance piece without live performers onstage was precocious evidence that Toda had caught the spirit of the time, in a country where performance was a lively, even a crucial, part of the art scene during the 1950s and 1960s.

Toda trained as an architect; though he has never built a building, he constructs the forms and sets in the pictures here. In their original settings, the architectural details or furnishings these photographs refer to—windows, altars, shrines—were fashioned to be long-lasting and functional. Toda takes artistic license with both their form and their function, destroying his constructions when the photography is finished, as if what he had made were a kind of performance architecture, as temporary as dance. The photography lives on as the work of art; the idea outlives its material expression.

Toda's materials are natural, simple, fundamental: wood, water, light, living creatures, in line with a long tradition of using simple materials in Japanese art, as well as a tradition of honoring the materials of one's crafts. His approach is both respectful and subdued: subdued color, strict geometries, careful symmetry, a studied tranquility.

The "Heian" project combines technical proficiency, an intense interest in the unique and fleeting moment, and considerable tenacity and patience—long waits and persistent endeavor to record a few transient seconds. Toda sets up strong challenges for himself, as if to make the work, its lucidity, and its apparent simplicity more potent by virtue of the time and effort that went into it.

The animals in these pictures were challenge enough. Toda researched them and traveled all over Japan looking for those he wanted, each to appear full size within the framework of the print (1030 x 728 or 1456 x 1030). The search had its obstacles. The frogs' eggs, for example, had to be found in remote, unpolluted places and photographed within three days of their appearance (a totally unpredictable date) before they changed shape.

All the creatures were alive and well when photographed but under almost any circumstance unlikely to sit still long enough to have their portraits made. (Getting a fish to stay upright and motionless even for a fraction of a second is doubtless more difficult than getting a nineteenth-century gentleman to keep his head still without an iron head brace.) They took sleeping pills for the occasion—the rabbit was the hardest case, as its ears inevitably drooped when it went to sleep—or, like the eruca (a kind of Japanese caterpillar), spent a short term in the refrigerator and, once outside again, had their pictures taken just as they began to move.

Each of Toda's live subjects, embodying and symbolic of life and change, has an extra significance: the species of fish and snake are popular in Japan, the metamorphosis of the frog is a wonder and a mystery, the silkworm is so precious that its export is prohibited by law, the eruca will metamorphose into a butterfly, the white rabbit and white pigeon symbolize peace. Only the crow is an object of fear: black as a demon, bringer of harm.

Toda also meticulously chooses the wood, a Japanese cedar called hinoki that is so responsive to sun and humidity that it rapidly changes color and cracks—a wood as subject to change as the living creatures it houses. This wood naturally varies in color as well as changing with age, but tricks of light also change our perception of it; the white shelves in several pictures are actually exactly the same pinkish shade as the adjacent wood but are photographed in direct light. The quality and angle of the light and the time of day were the most important elements of all in the making of these pictures, each taken on a cloudy day at midday when there were no shadows. It is not hard to believe Toda when he says it takes about a year to make four pieces.

No doubt there were times when he cursed the sun, but his time and effort have been spent in search of an atmosphere as natural and gentle as the creatures in it, an atmosphere suffused with light and tender color, where even living creatures hold still enough to be converted to pure form, to become an element in a strict, stripped-down, formally pure invitation to meditation. Toda refers to the spareness of these images, the total lack of any distracting element, as *subtraction*, an Asiatic attitude to art that involves finding the way to beauty with the barest of means.

After all his labor, he subtracts again, taking only one picture of each subject. (Or to be exact, directing only one picture of each subject.) The resulting images are singularly still evocations of evanescent (if not improbable) moments, as still and quiet as some unlikely eternity. This nice little paradox, which has some analogs in Western-constructed photography, has an extra resonance in Japan, where impermanence, flux, fluidity, concepts the West was long rather afraid of, are built into the notion of time. In Japan, time is not regarded as linear, as it often is in the West, but as a state of becoming, a series of suspended moments, a constant and fluctuating present. As early as *The Tale of Genji*, written in the Heian period (784–1185 A.D.), the transitory nature of things and of life itself was regarded as having a melancholy beauty.

Some of these images are quietly, quizzically humorous: What is venison doing on a ladder? Why are a deer and a rabbit wearing armor vaguely reminiscent of the armor of ancient Japan, unless it is to say that these animals could use some protection? If you think about it, it is also a bit strange for a fish to be posing in profile for its portrait, not to mention a bee or a caterpillar.

In the years following the Second World War, and indeed still today, Japanese artists reacted against the dominance of the modernist Western tradition in Japanese contemporary art. Many artists consciously sought a means of making modern art on specifically Japanese terms, attempting to accomplish this by including and referring to Japanese traditions.

Seiju Toda's work can be placed in this stream. The use of a traditional Japanese wooden tub and a metal bucket in his high school performance already demonstrated an interest in marrying Japanese and western traditions in the context of modern art. In the Heian project, he not only refers to Buddhist altars, Japanese alcoves, and folding screens, but also uses a Japanese wood, Japanese or Chinese creatures, and a traditional Asiatic approach to space.

He insists that he does not focus on old Japan. These pictures make no specific reference to the Heian period but reflect his idea of it as a shadowless time, a time of quiet gardens and gentle architecture and a pervasive sense of naturalness. He is fully aware of the historic past of Japanese art, which is obviously dear to him, but far from copying or resurrecting ancient tradition, he pays it homage in the context of modern formal abstraction and conceptual art.

Several of these pictures play with spatial perception. The eye-like cavities that house the silk worms tilt a bit or seem to be set into convex shapes; in fact they are on folding screens. In the Ranchu pictures (a Ranchu is a rare and expensive Chinese fish, prized by collectors), boundaries are eliminated, producing bands of pale color that span the width of the picture, a nod to abstract geometric paintings á la Gene Davis or Elsworth Kelly.

Lighting is so even that recession sometimes virtually disappears. In the image called "Ranchu Red" with its three fish, the slight changes in size are the only reliable clues to the fact that the fish are actually on steps that go back as well as up. We know in our minds that what we see cannot be flat, but eye and mind end up fighting over the matter, for vision suggests a space without depth. The general effect is close to the rendition of space in traditional Japanese painting, where objects and people at a distance from the forward plane are placed *above* those that are nearer to the spectator.

Toda expressly says that he wants to remove himself from his images, which do not showcase his personal opinions or emotions. He says he simply wants to show what is there as it is. This removal of the self is distinctly Asian, having its origins in Buddhism, which considers detachment from the world an ideal state, and it has been a strong element in Japanese art at least since the Heian period. Haiku, for instance, often speak more to the essence of an object or scene than to the emotions of the poet.

In fact the overt expression of individuality, generally credited to the Renaissance in the West, is a fairly recent development in Japanese art and goes against the grain of a culture that puts the community above the individual. Indifference as an artistic posture was imported into Western art when nineteenth-century artists like Manet discovered Japanese prints and paintings. In the twentieth century, Duchamp and Warhol were the prime examples, but conceptual and minimalist artists made certain that the idea stayed alive.

Not that Toda is without opinions or ideas about what his pictures represent. (Nor can he quite help himself; an individual sensibility shines through in his work despite the distance and impersonality he imposes on the imagery.) The minimal nature of these scenes is itself a call to the viewer's imagination, a field for the mind to play on. Toda's hope is that his images will, by virtue of the simplicity of their means, materials, and living creatures, arouse in viewers an awareness of environmental problems and of the overarching need for peace and the continuation of life.

Peace is a pervasive theme in this work. The title word, "Heian," the name of a period of courtly sophistication and nostalgic sentiment, is composed of two ideographs, one signifying peace and the other calmness or serenity. Toda's meditative call to peace expresses a hope but not a direction; he says, "I don't mind at all if viewers get other feelings from my works. Whatever they feel is up to the individual."

So, in effect, the viewer completes the pictures, as happens with all photographs. Here are the images, puzzling, amusing, tranquil, and pure, open invitations to the eye and mind.

BAR. Plain Wood, Red Roundfish (1456 × 1030)

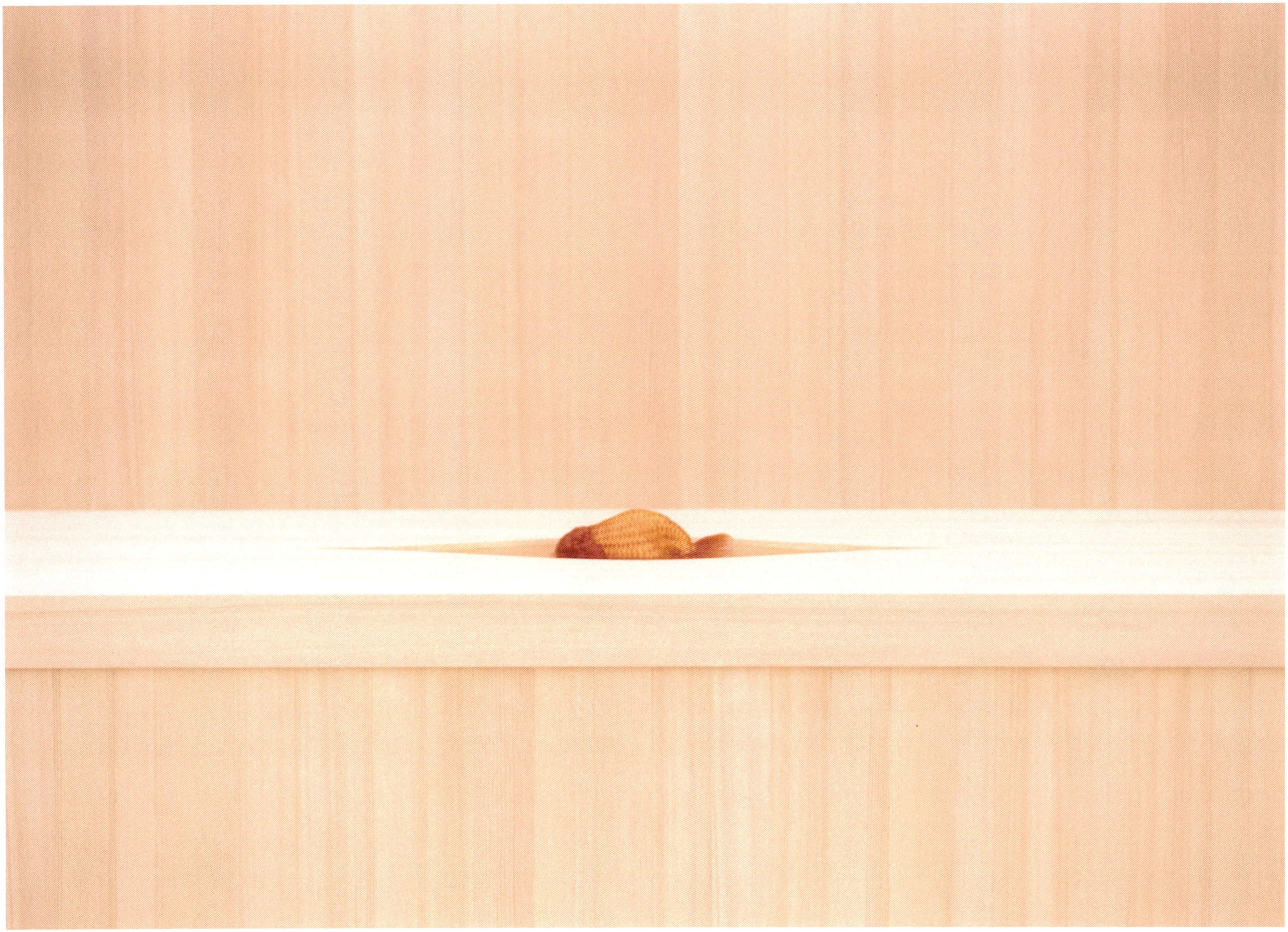

STAIRS. Plain Wood, Red Roundfishes (1456 × 1030)

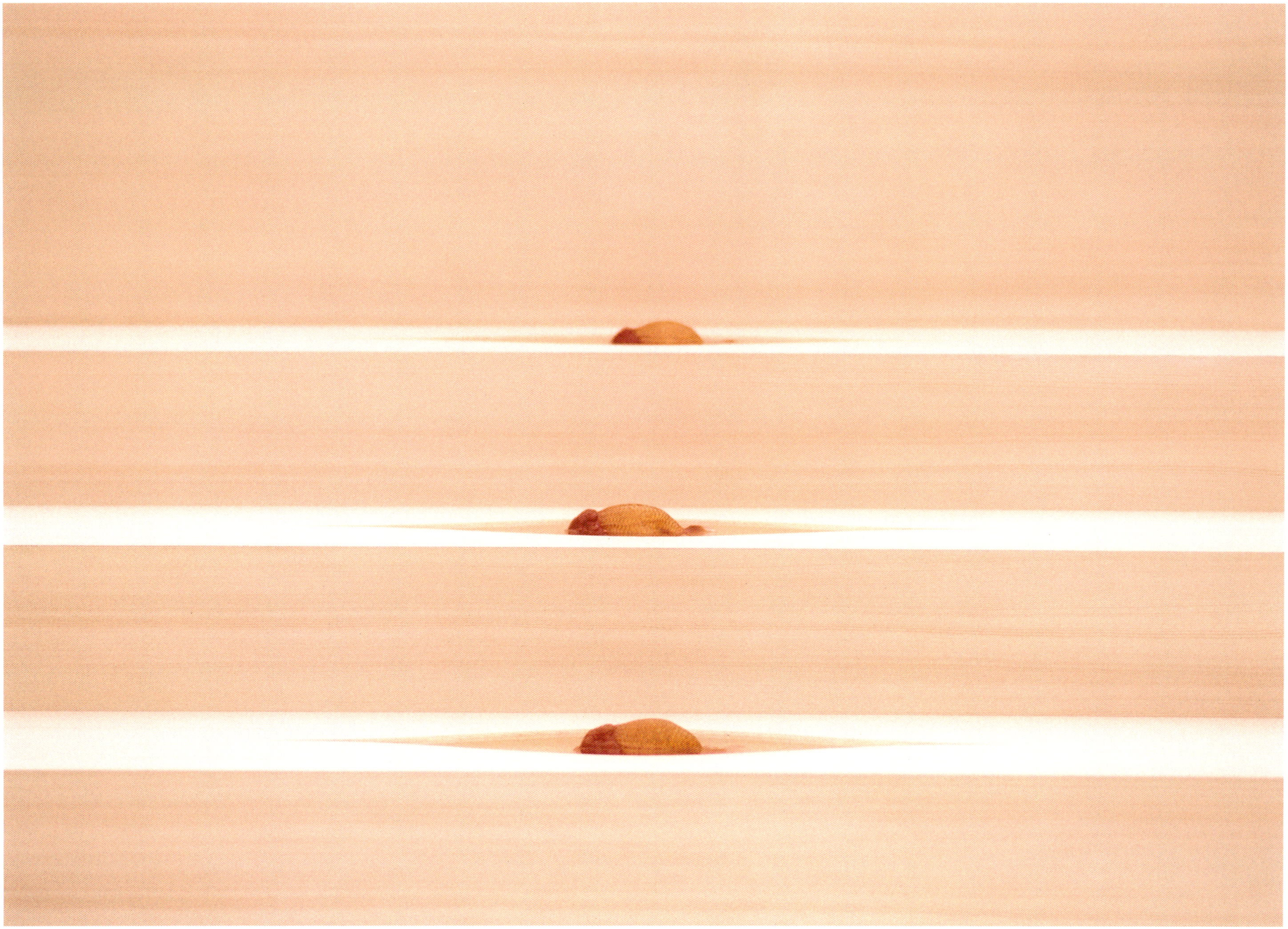

FOLDING SCREEN. Plain Wood, Silkworms (1456 × 1030)

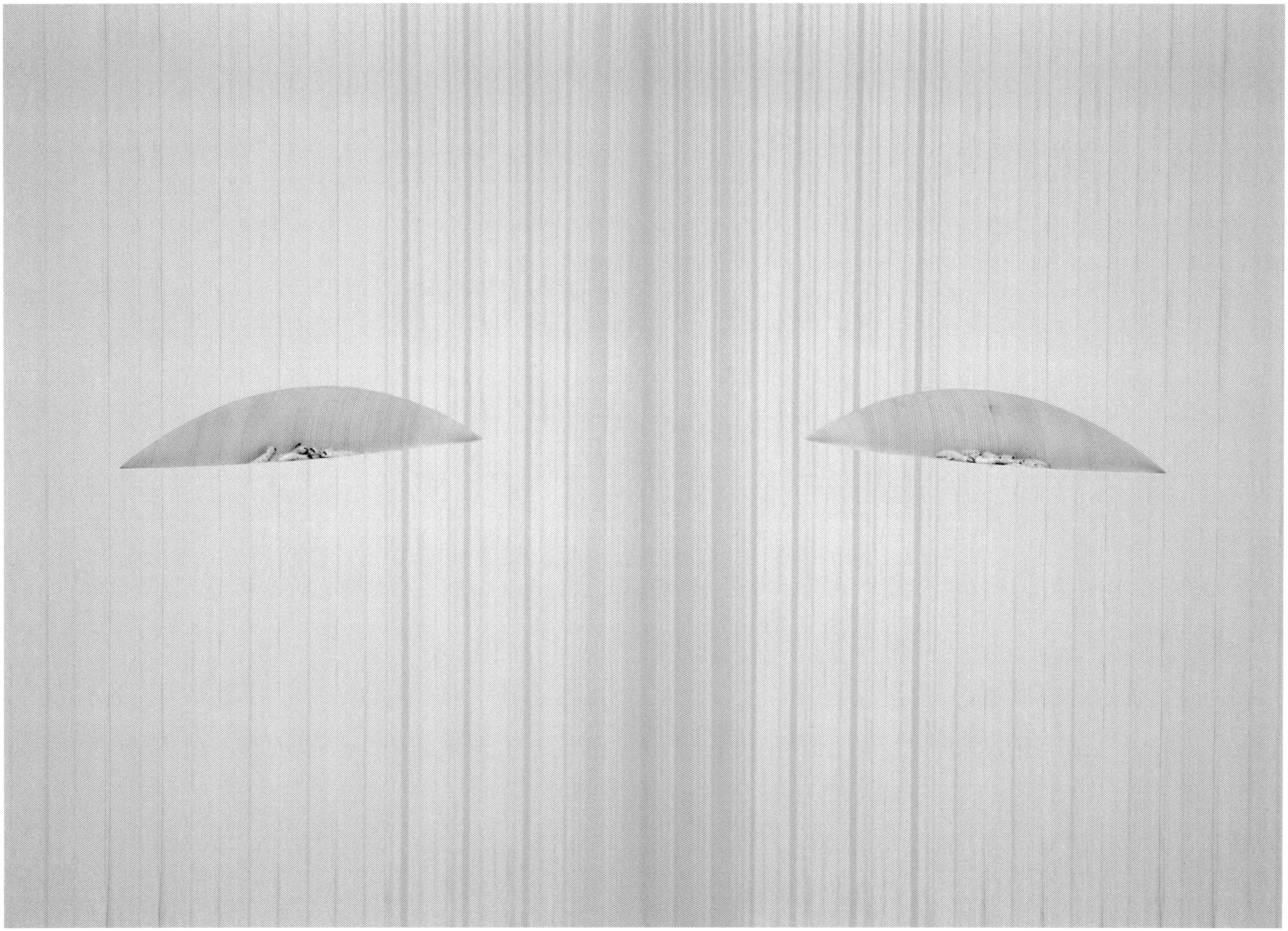

FOLDING SCREEN. Plain Wood, Silkworms (1456 × 1030)

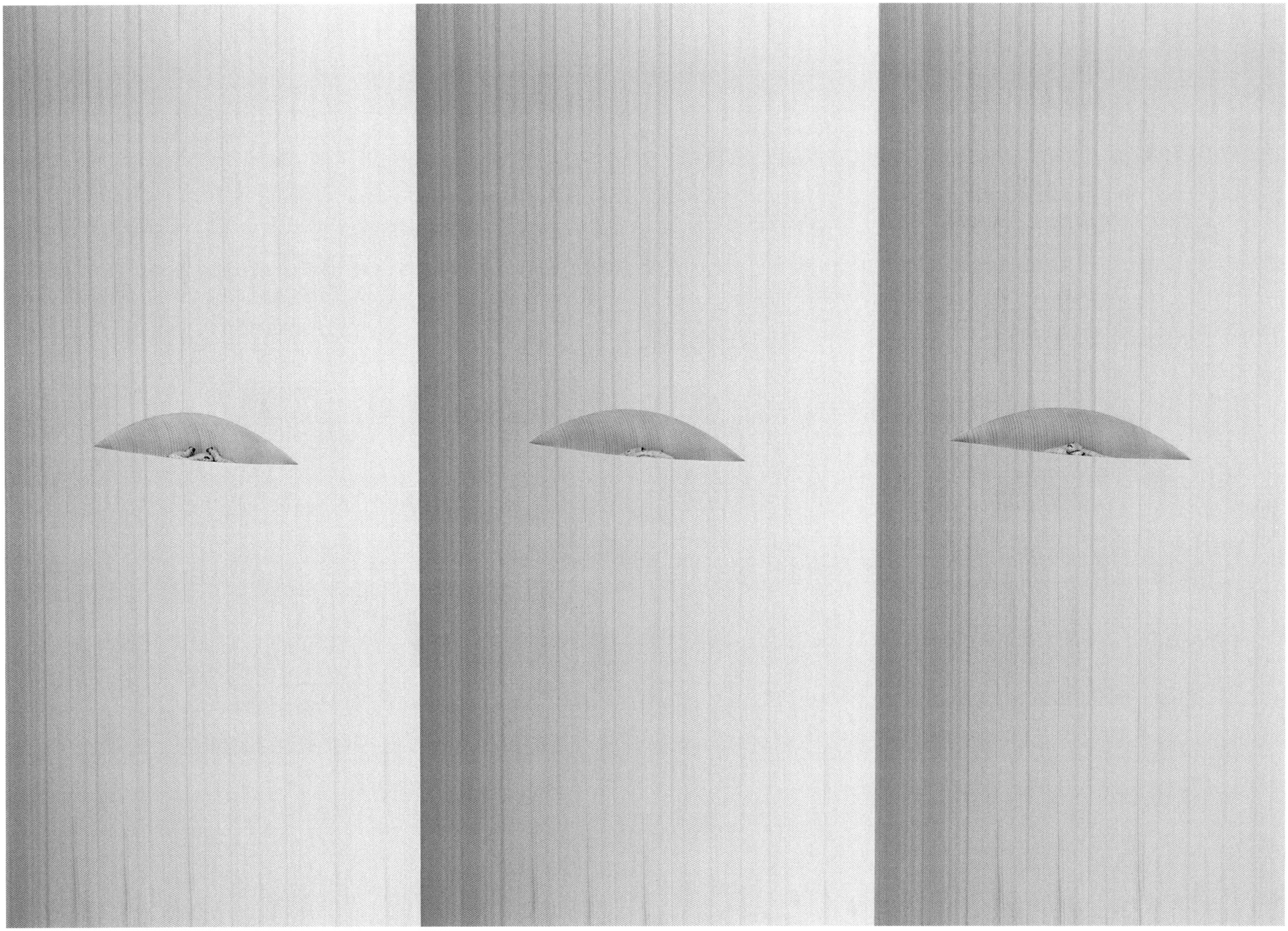

RAIL. Plain Wood partly lacquered, Black Carps (1456 × 1030)

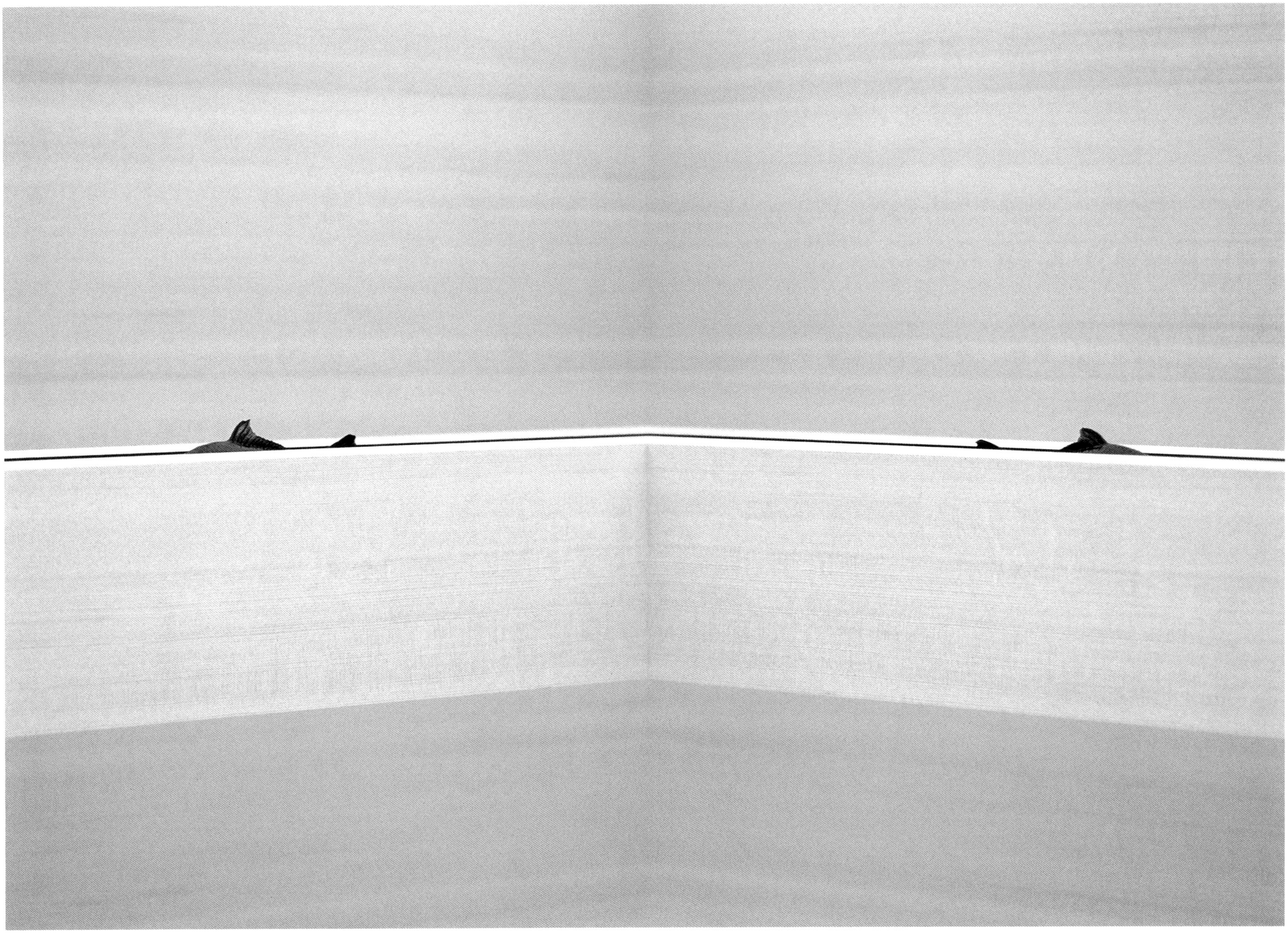

RAIL. Plain Wood partly lacquered, Black Carps (1456 × 1030)

FANLIGHT. Plain Wood, Erucas (1456 × 1030)

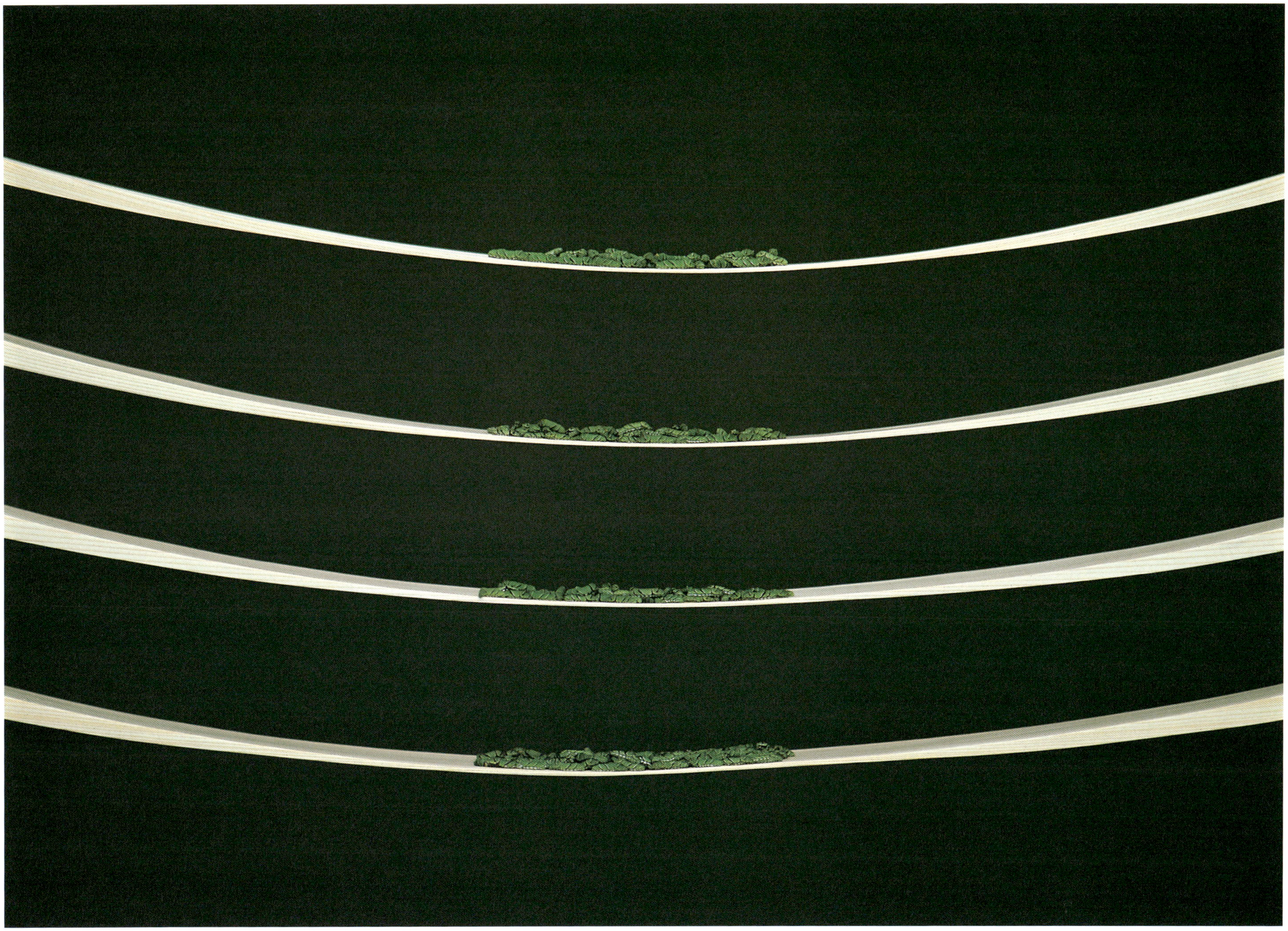

LANTERN. Plain Wood, Erucas (1456 × 1030)

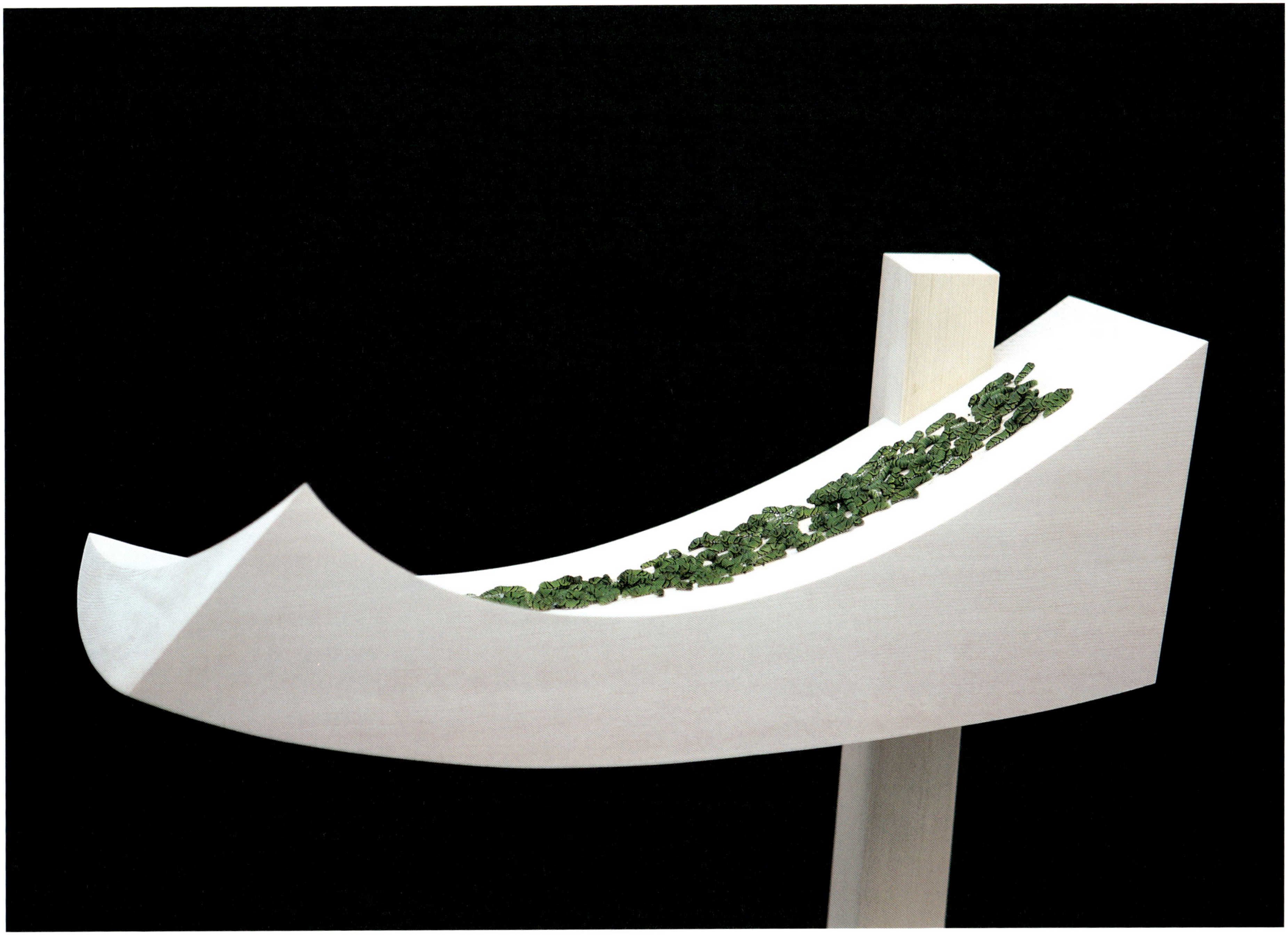

FANLIGHT. Plain Wood, Bees (1456 × 1030)

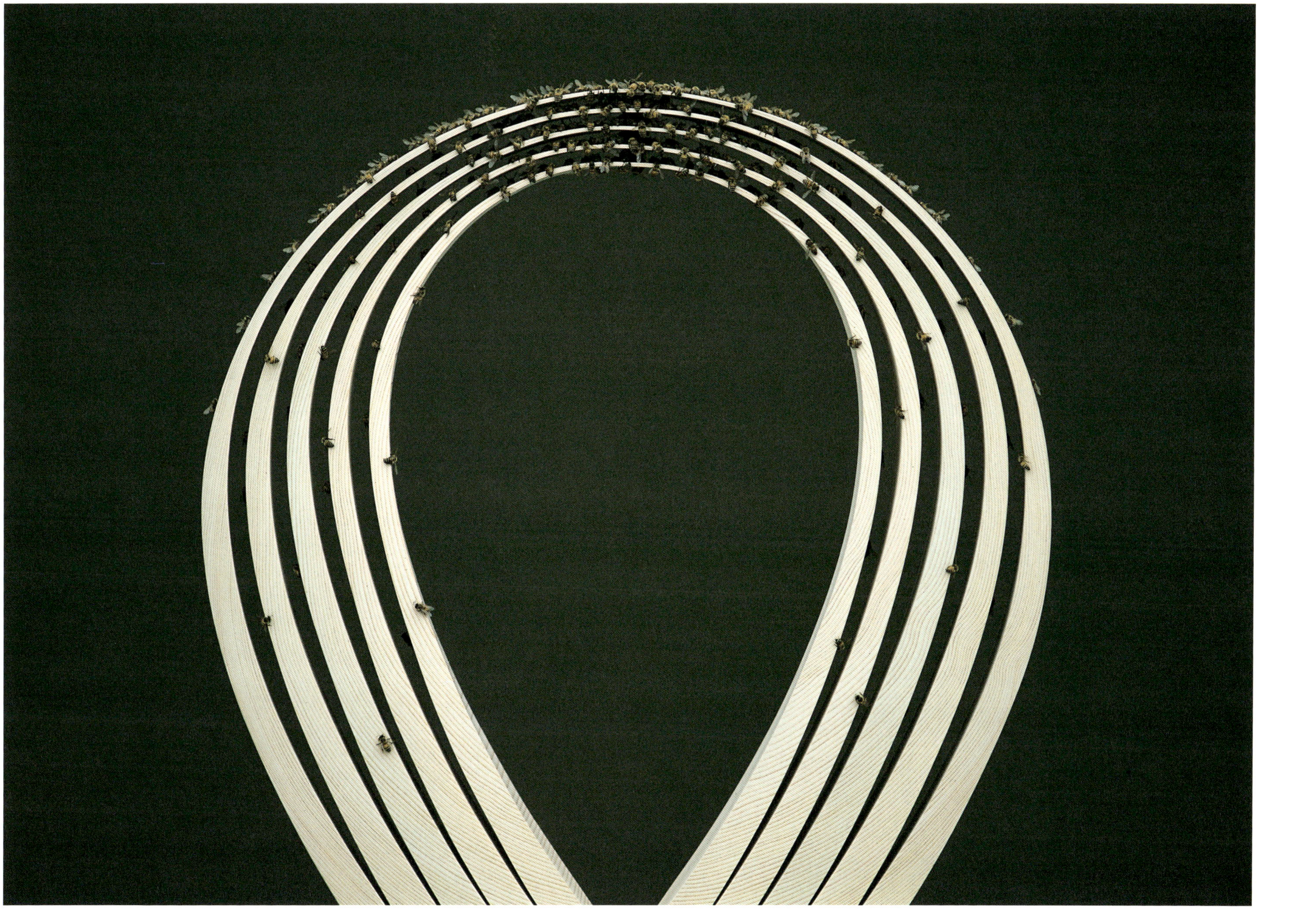

BATH ROOM. Plain Wood partly gilded, White Carps (1456 × 1030)

BATH ROOM. Plain Wood partly gilded, White Carp (1456 × 1030)

TABLE. Plain Wood partly lacquered, Ray (1030 × 728)

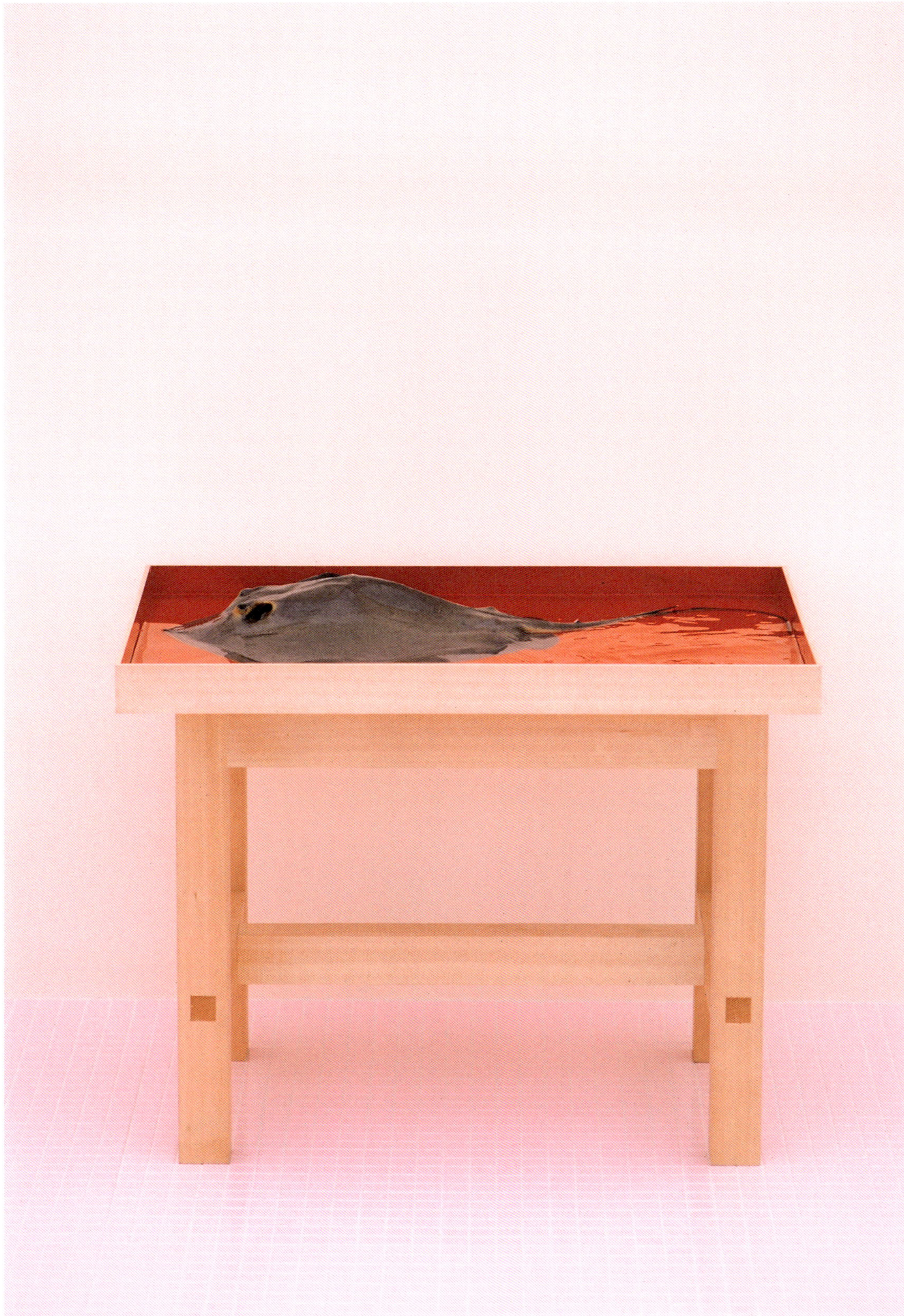

LADDER. Plain Wood partly lacquered, Red Carps (1030 × 728)

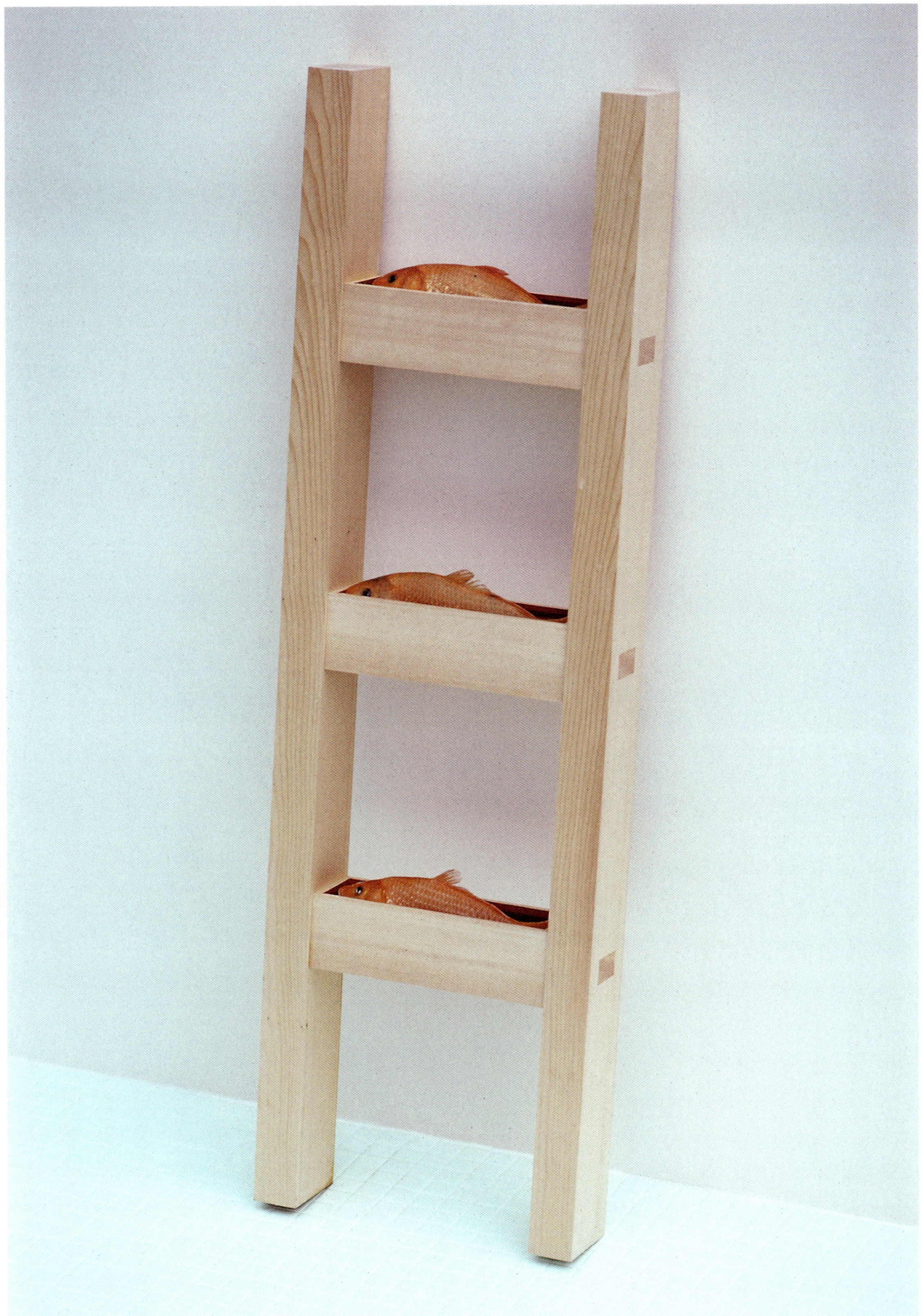

BOOKSHELF. Plain Wood partly lacquered, Slices of Venison (1030 × 728)

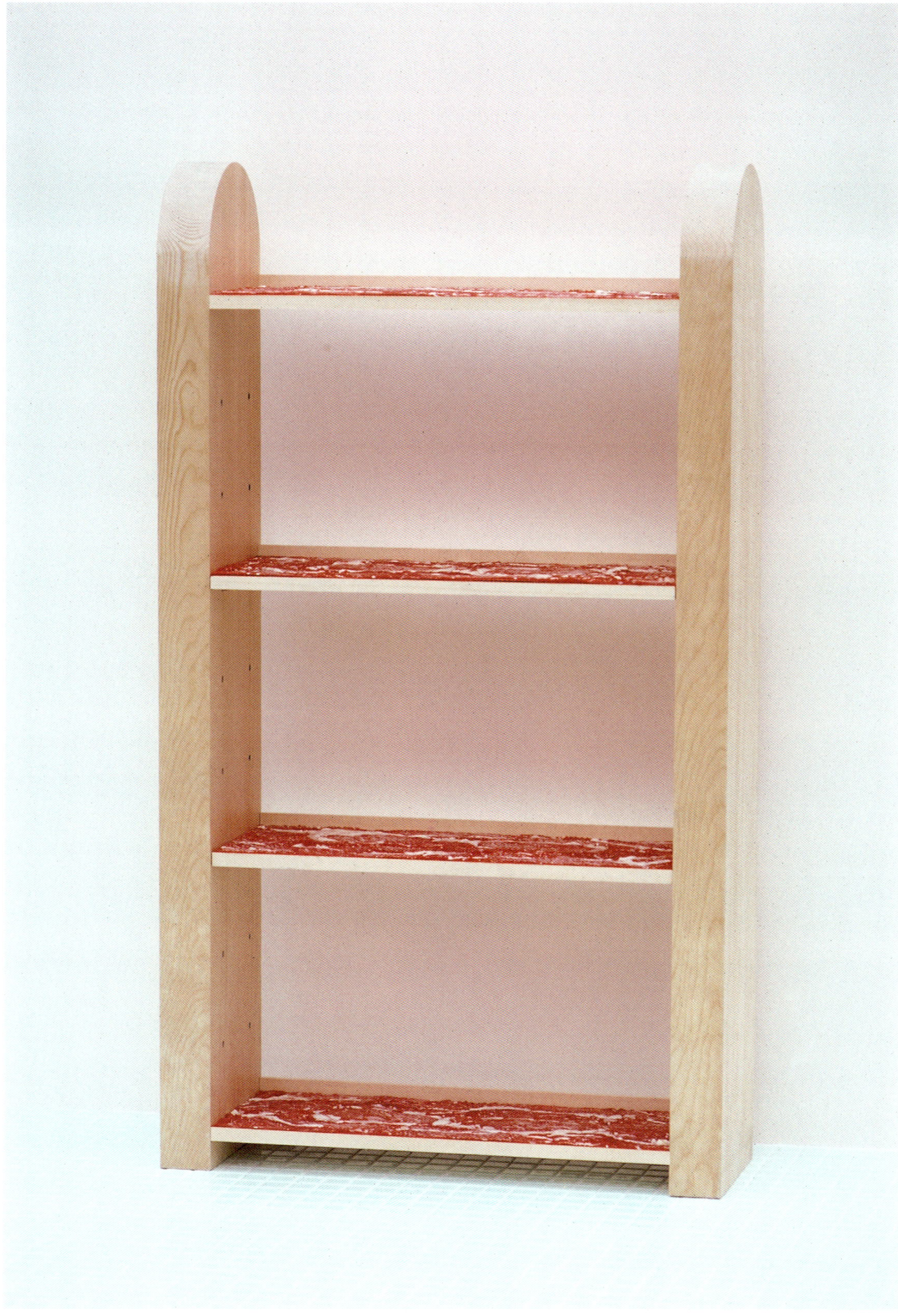

ALCOVE. Plain Wood, White and Red Roundfish (1456 × 1030)

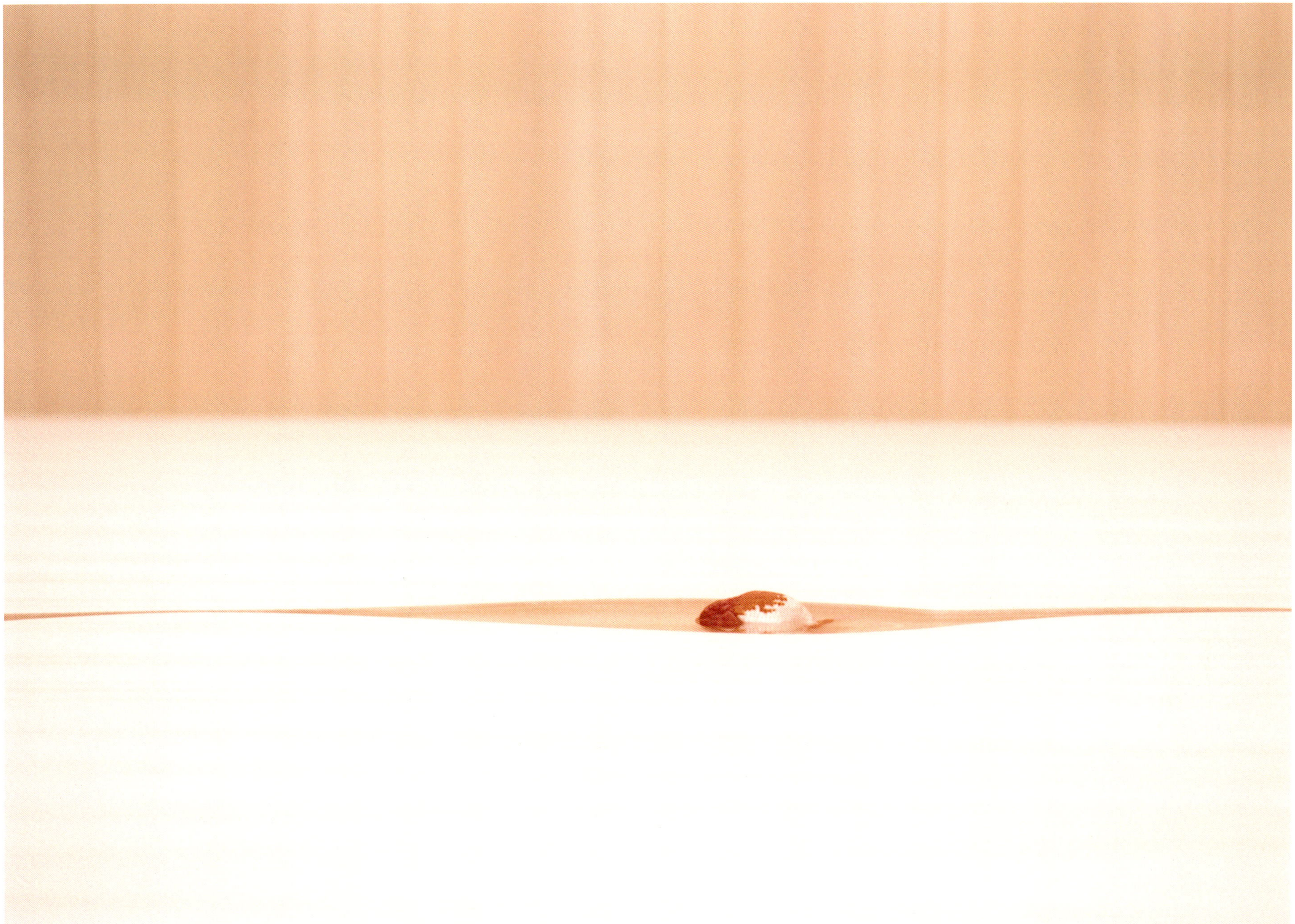

ALCOVE. Plain Wood, White and Red Roundfish (1456 × 1030)

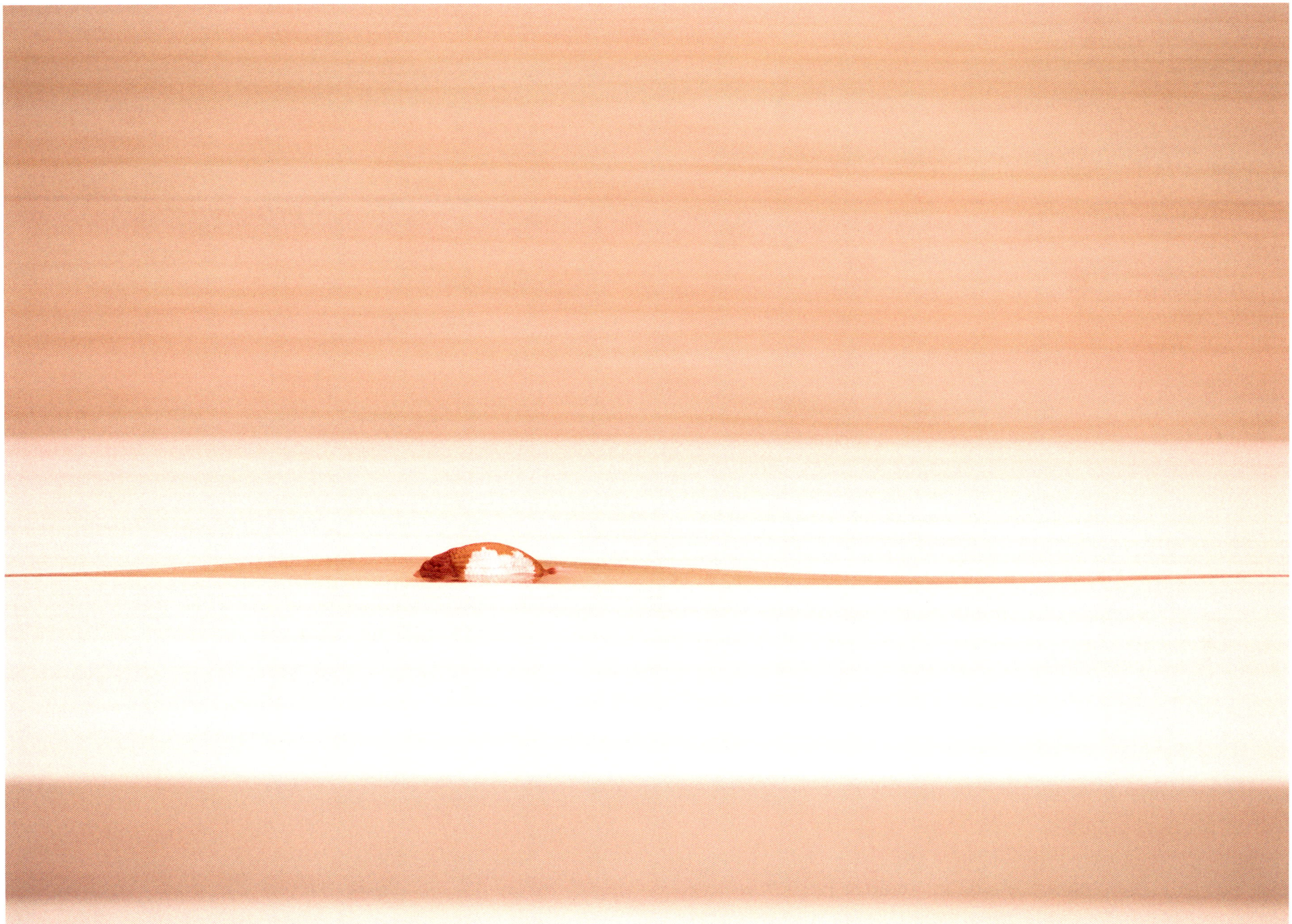

SUNKEN HEARTH. Plain Wood partly gilded, White Carps (1456 × 1030)

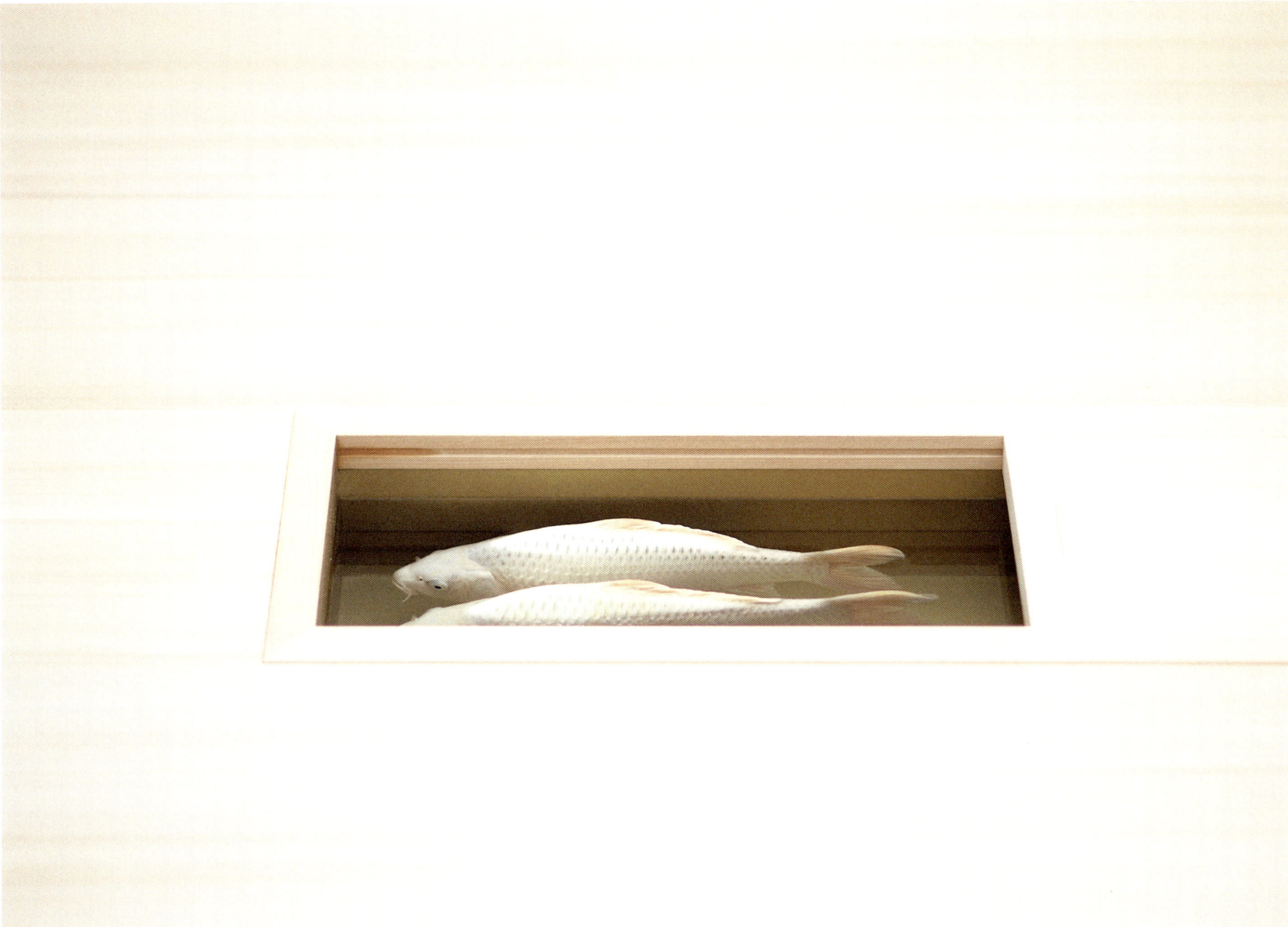

SUNKEN HEARTH. Plain Wood partly gilded, Bamboo, White Carp (1456 × 1030)

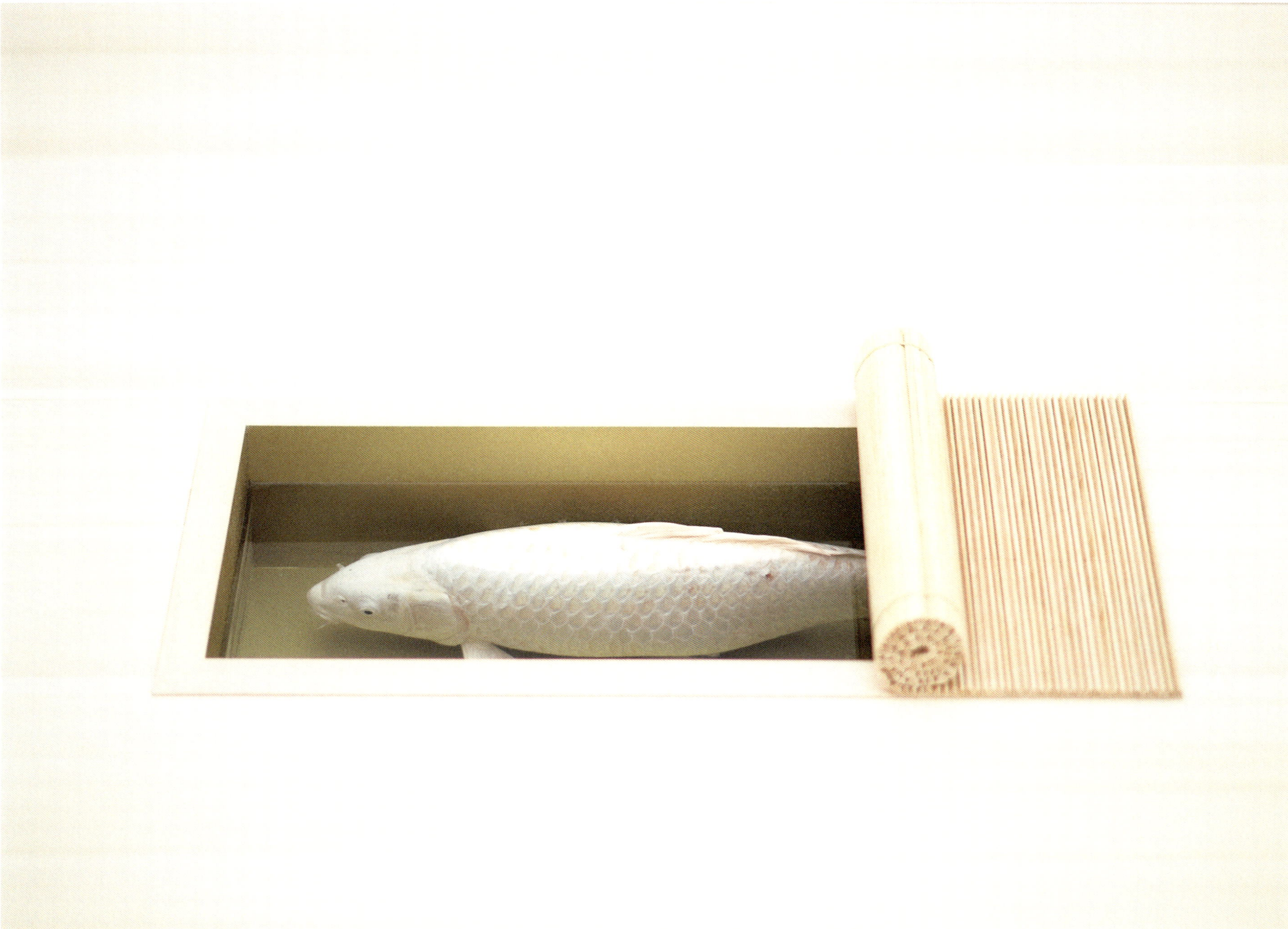

WATER BASIN. Plain Wood, Frog Eggs (1456 × 1030)

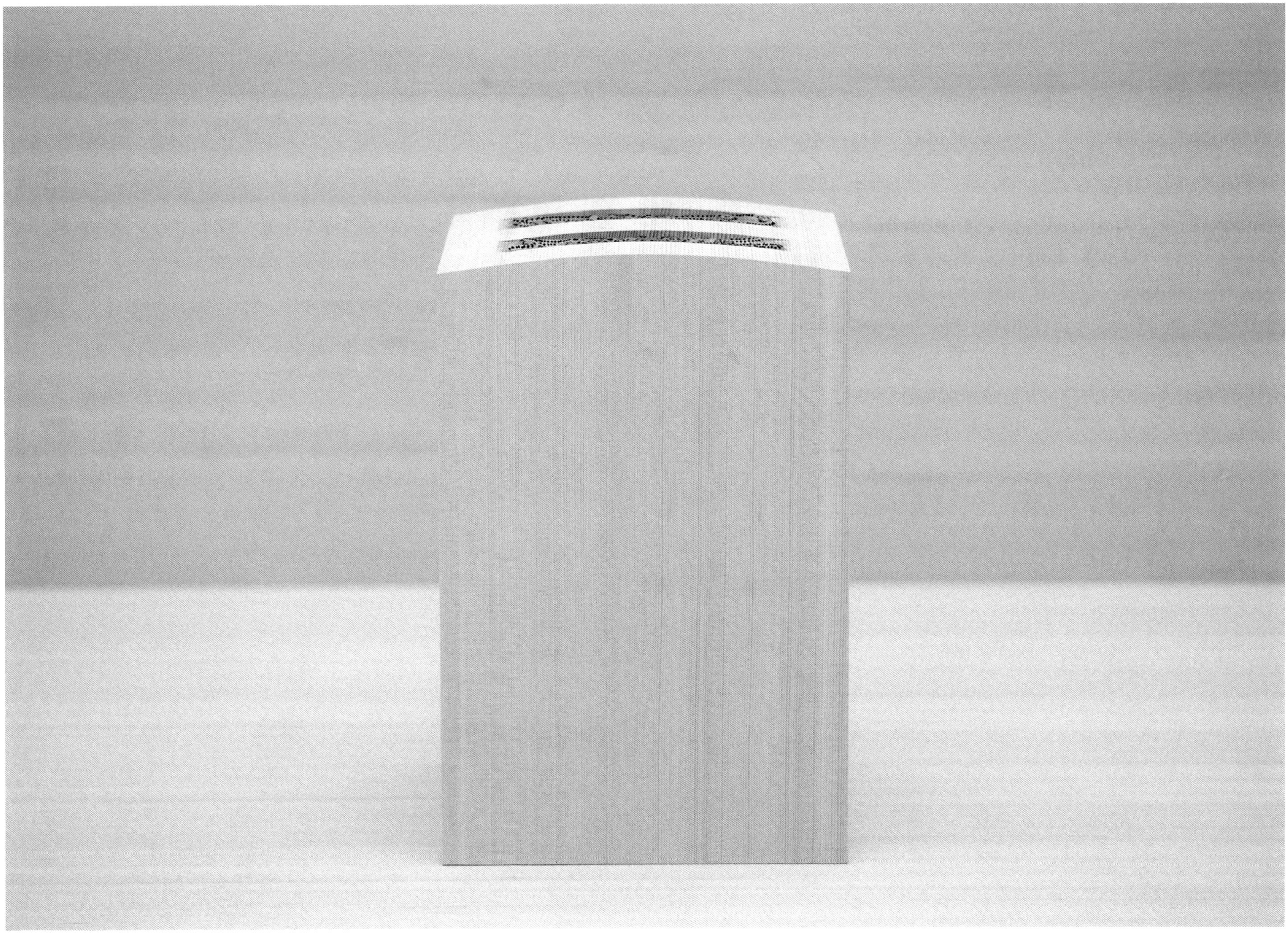

WATER BASIN. Plain Wood, Frog Eggs (1456 × 1030)

SHELF. Plain Wood partly gouached, Frog Eggs (1456 × 1030)

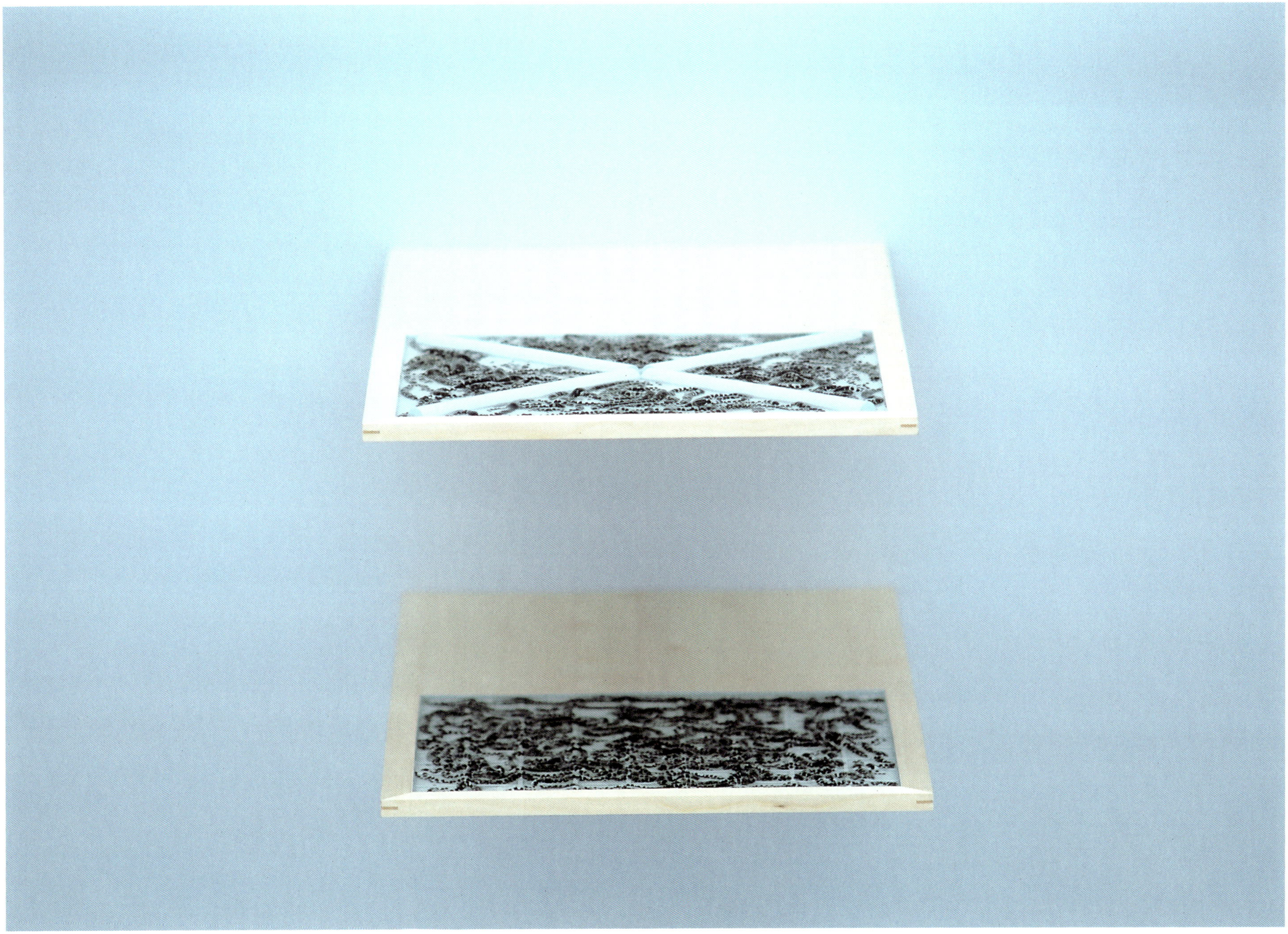

SHELF. Plain Wood partly gouached, Frog Eggs (1456 × 1030)

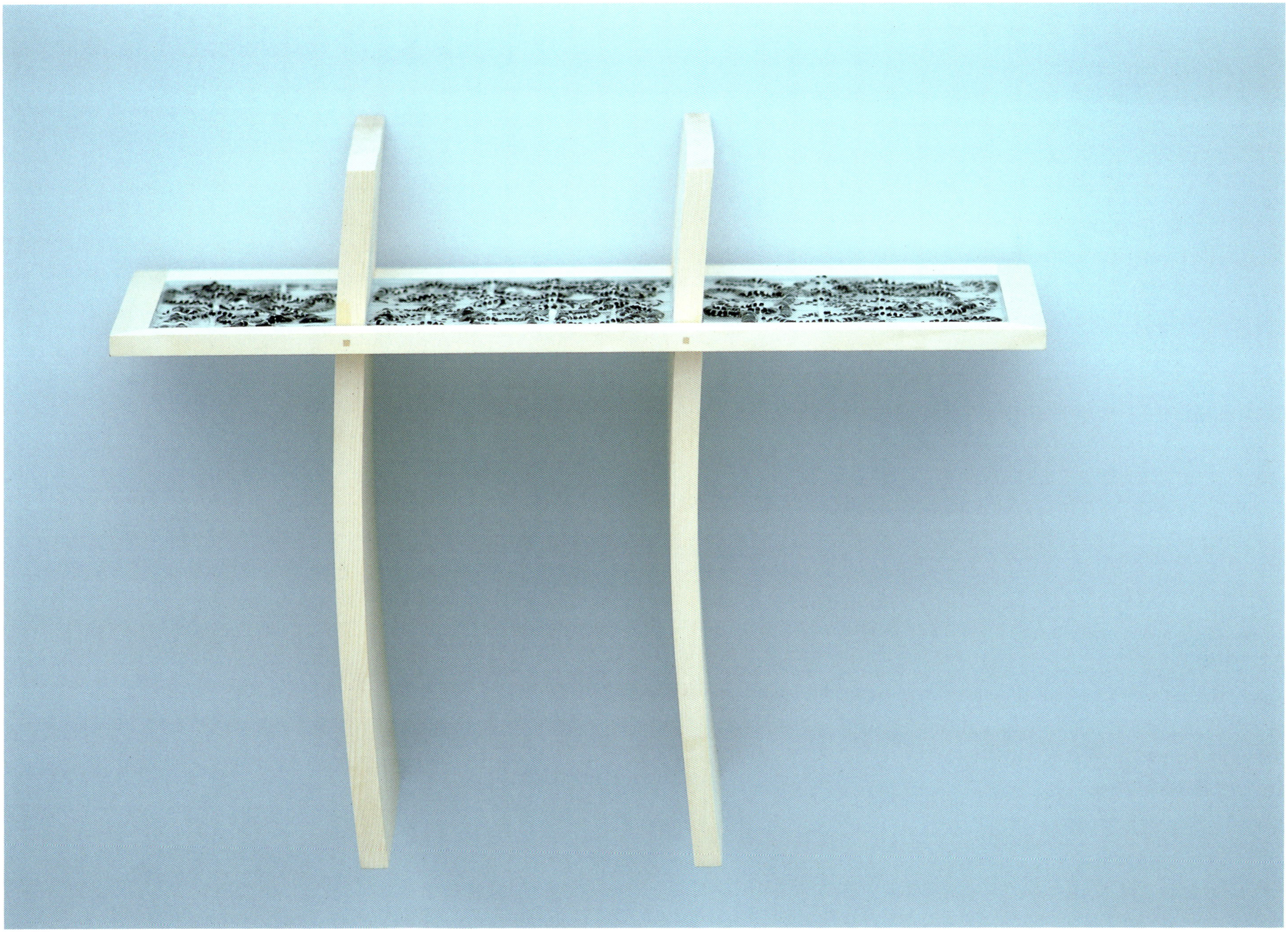

ARMOR. Plain Wood, Rabbit (1456 × 1030)

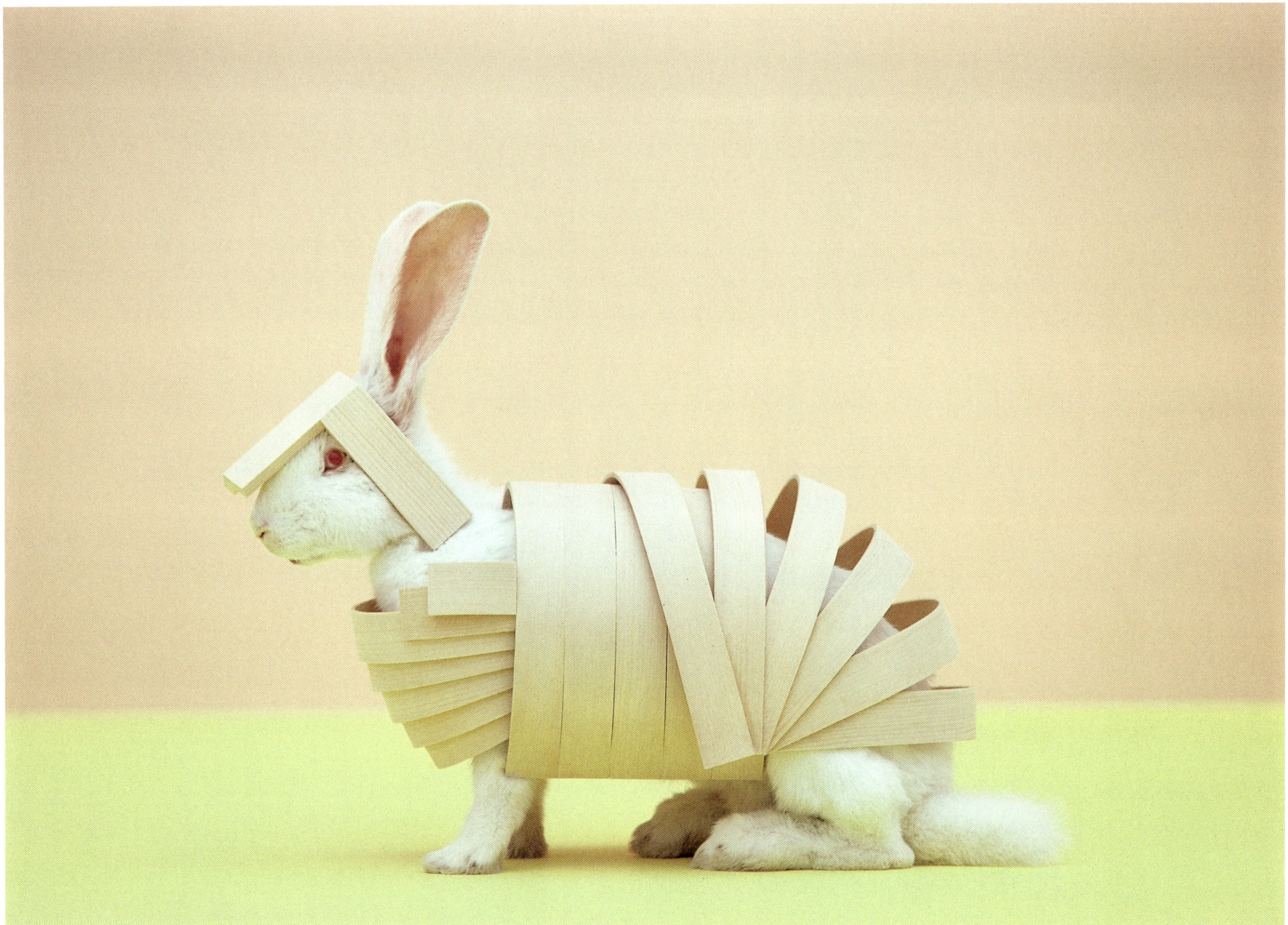

ARMOR. Plain Wood, Deer (1456 × 1030)

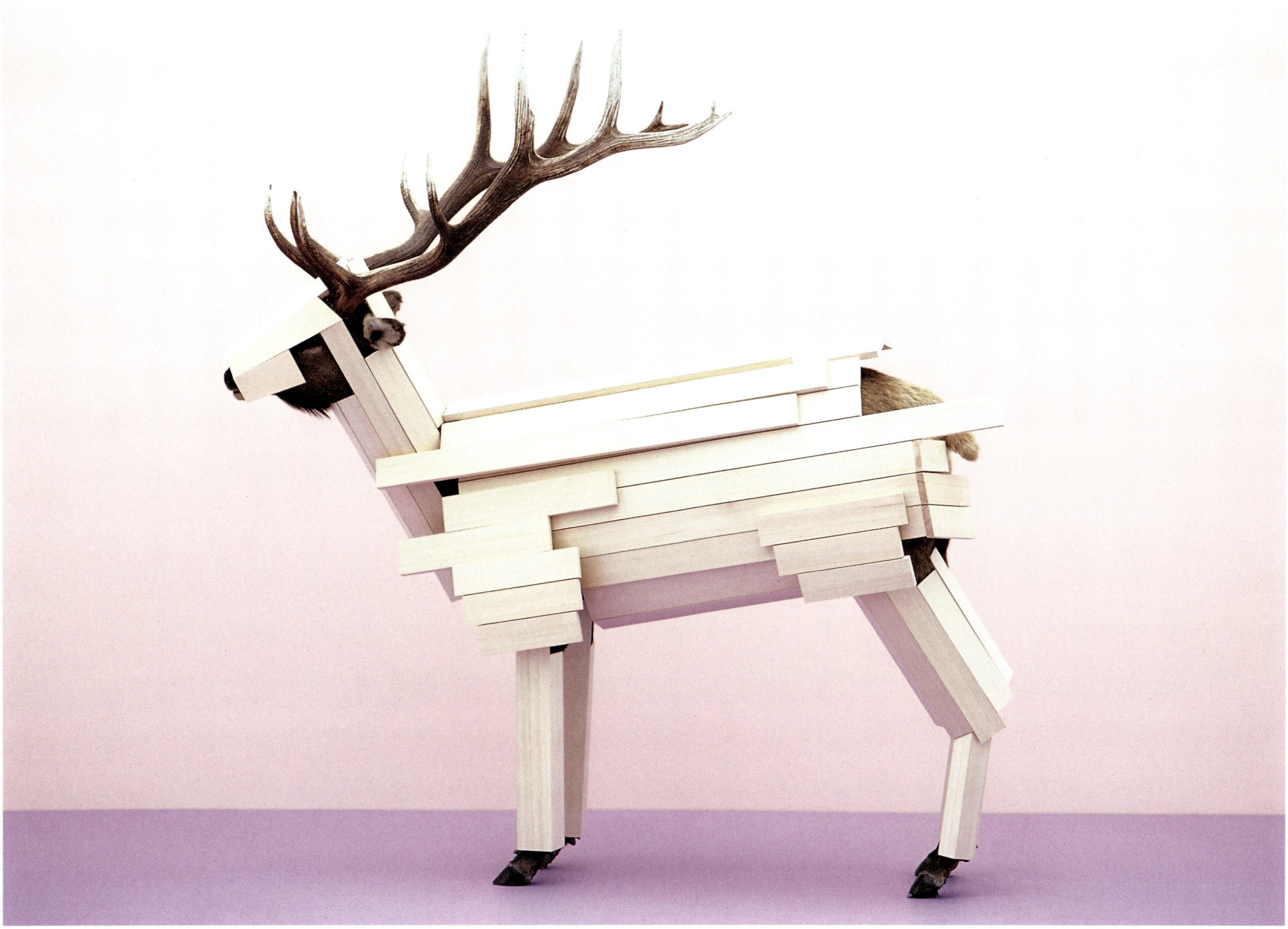

YUKAWAKIDANA (Rack in an alcove). Plain Wood, White Pigeon (1456 × 1030)

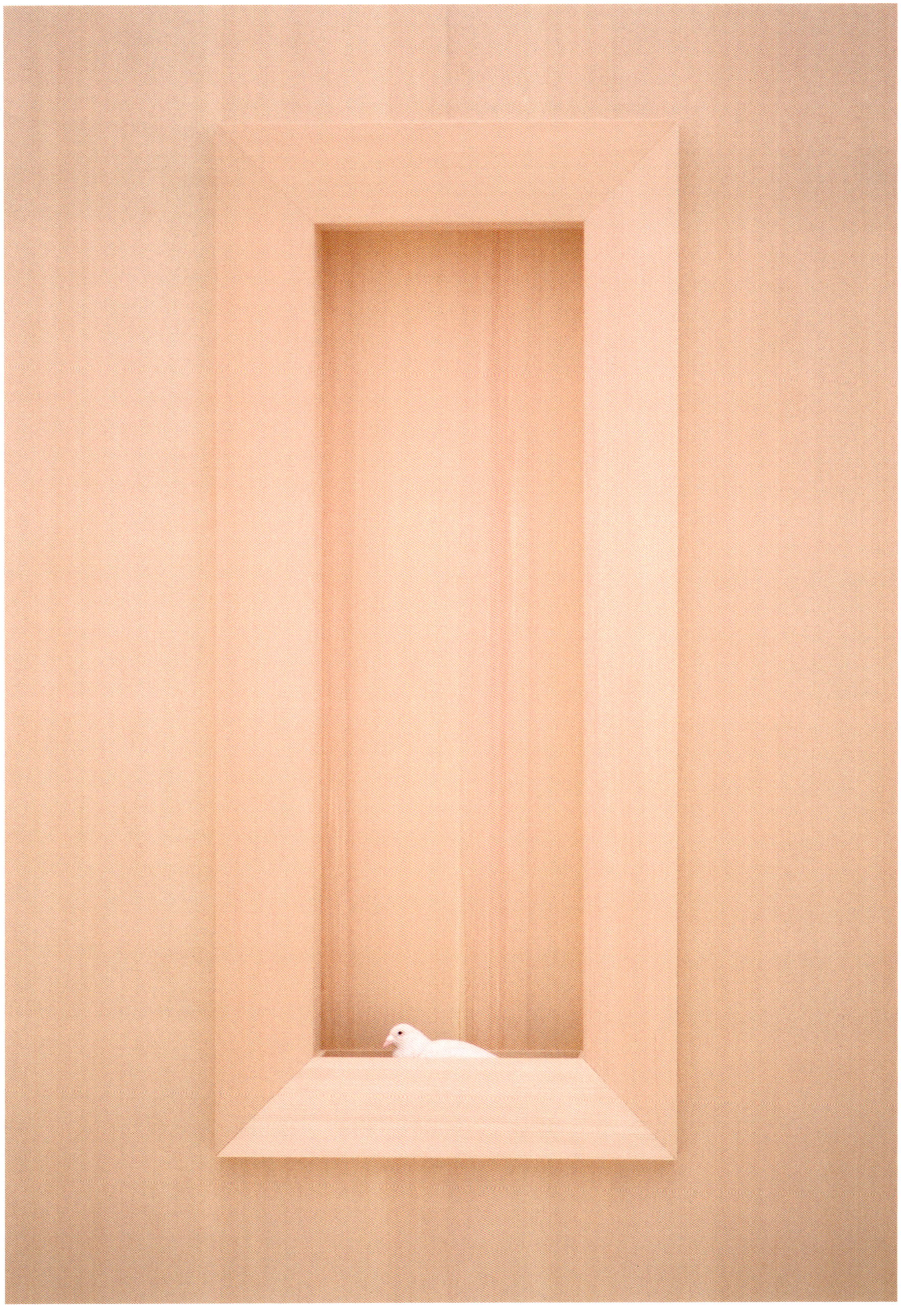

YUKAWAKIDANA (Rack in an alcove). Plain Wood, White Pigeons (1456 × 1030)

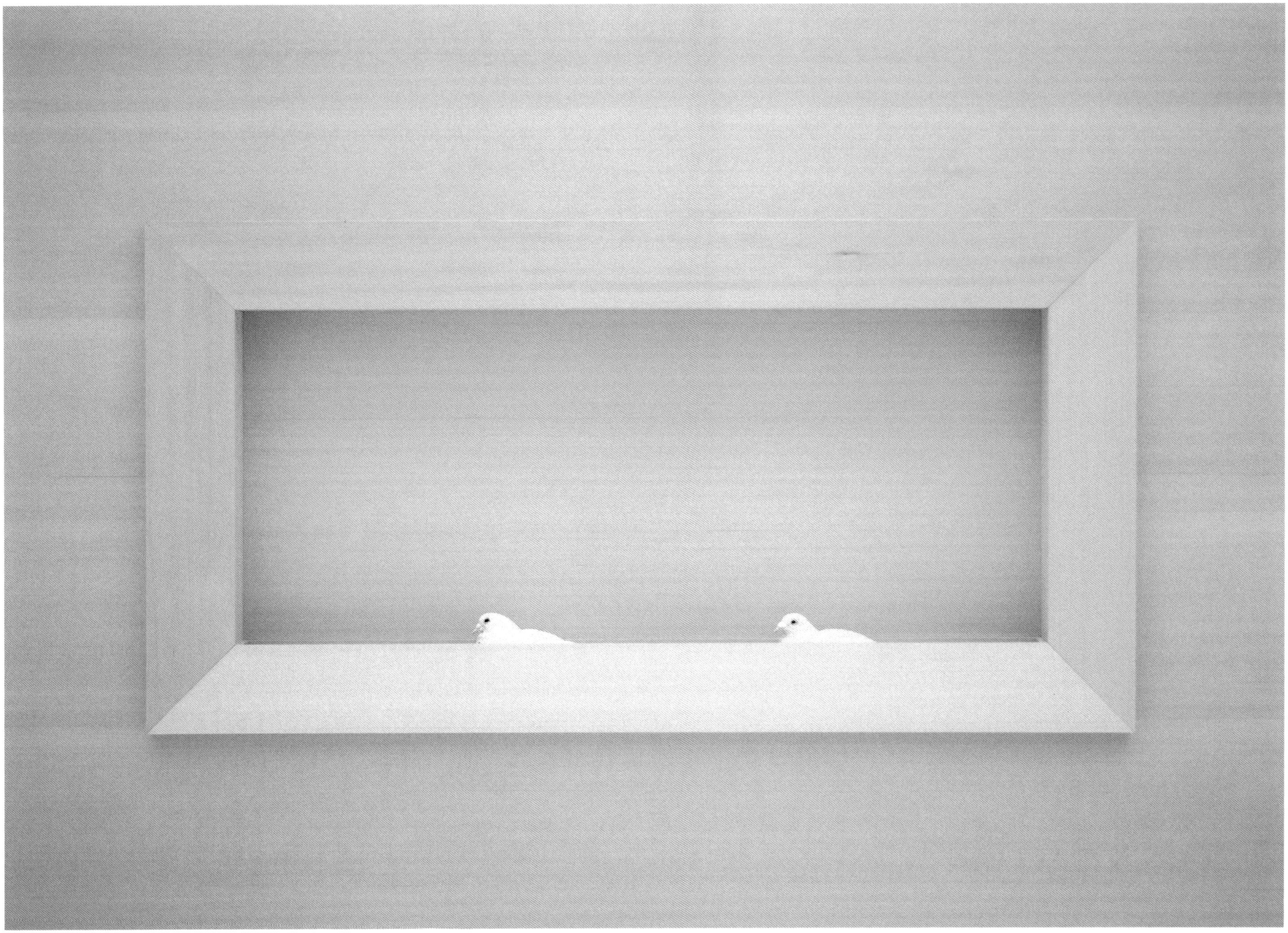

SHITAJIMADO (Window on the clay wall). Plain Wood partly gilded, Snakes (1456 × 1030)

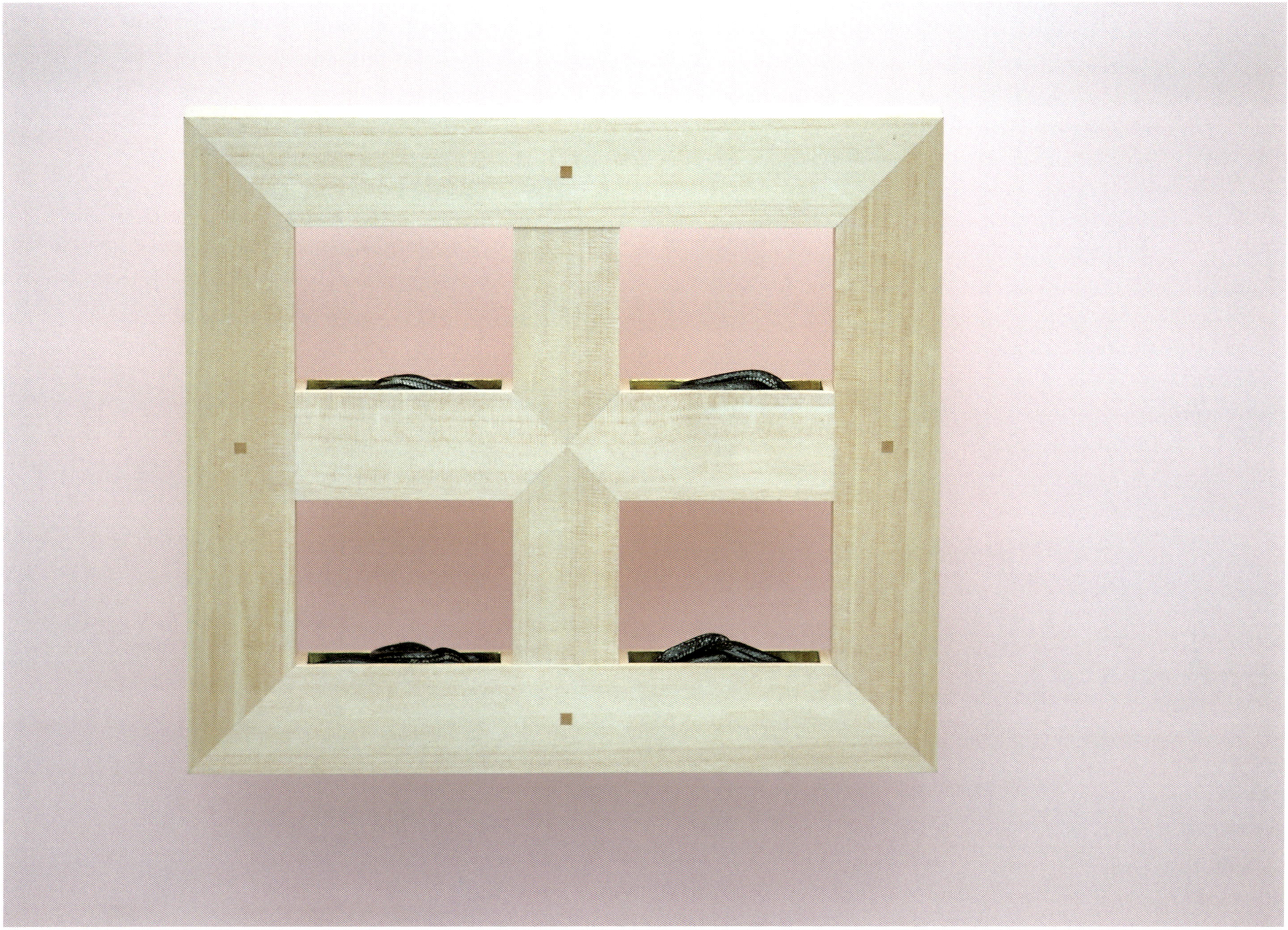

ALCOVE POST. Plain Wood partly gilded, Snakes (1456 × 1030)

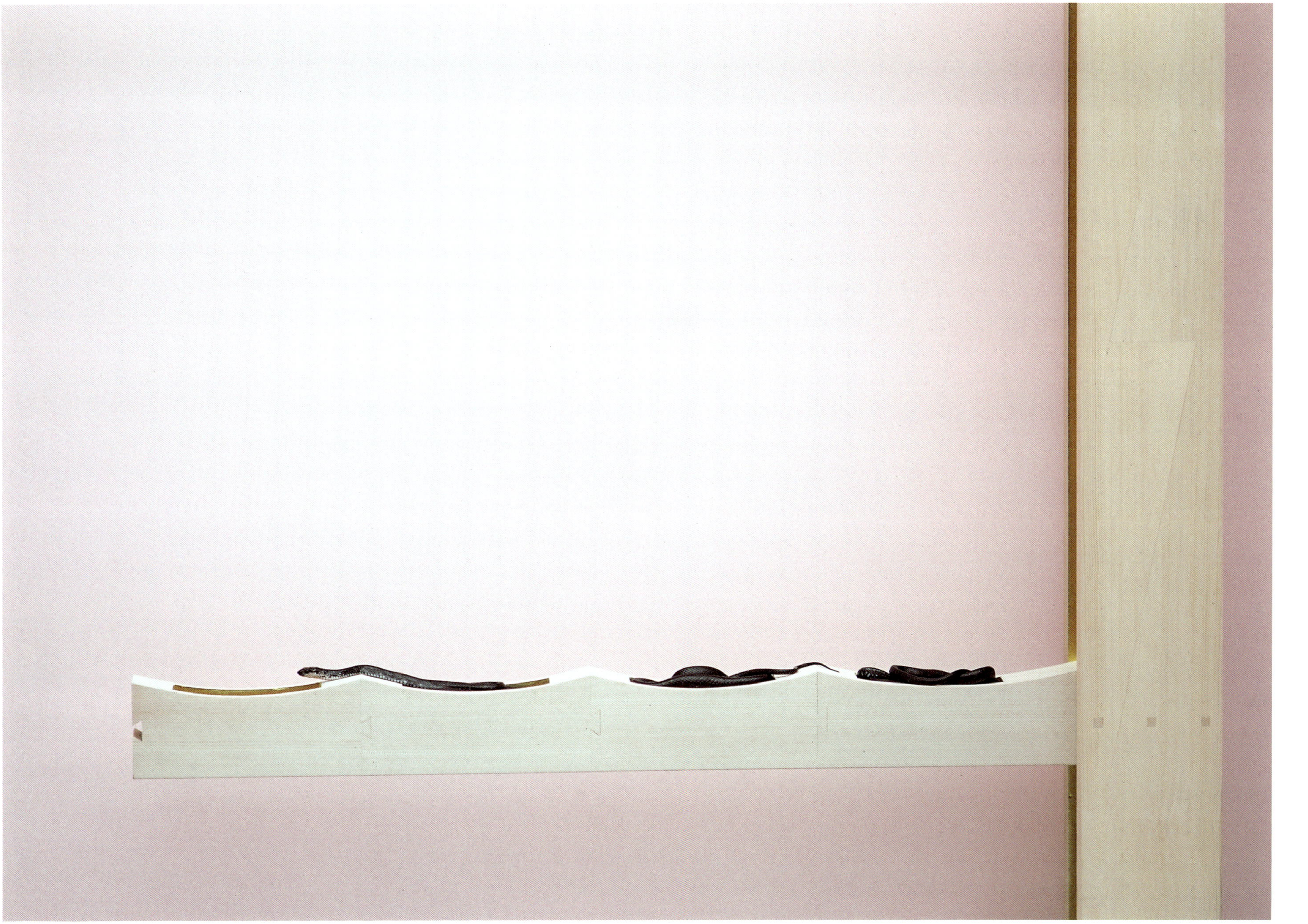

ARMOR. Plain Wood, Snakes (1456 × 1030)

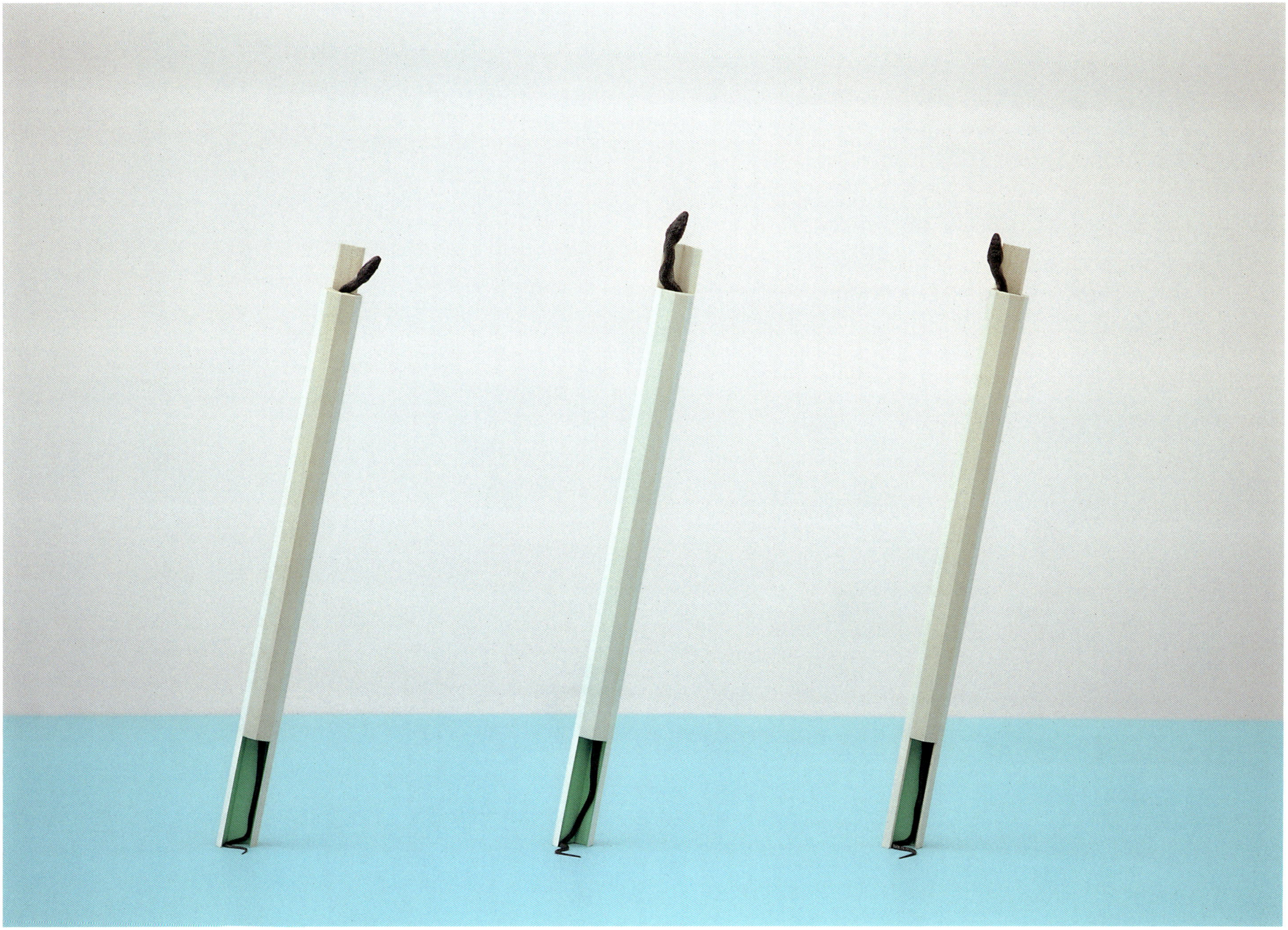

CHIBUKURO (Low cabinet). Plain Wood, Crucian Carps (1456 × 1030)

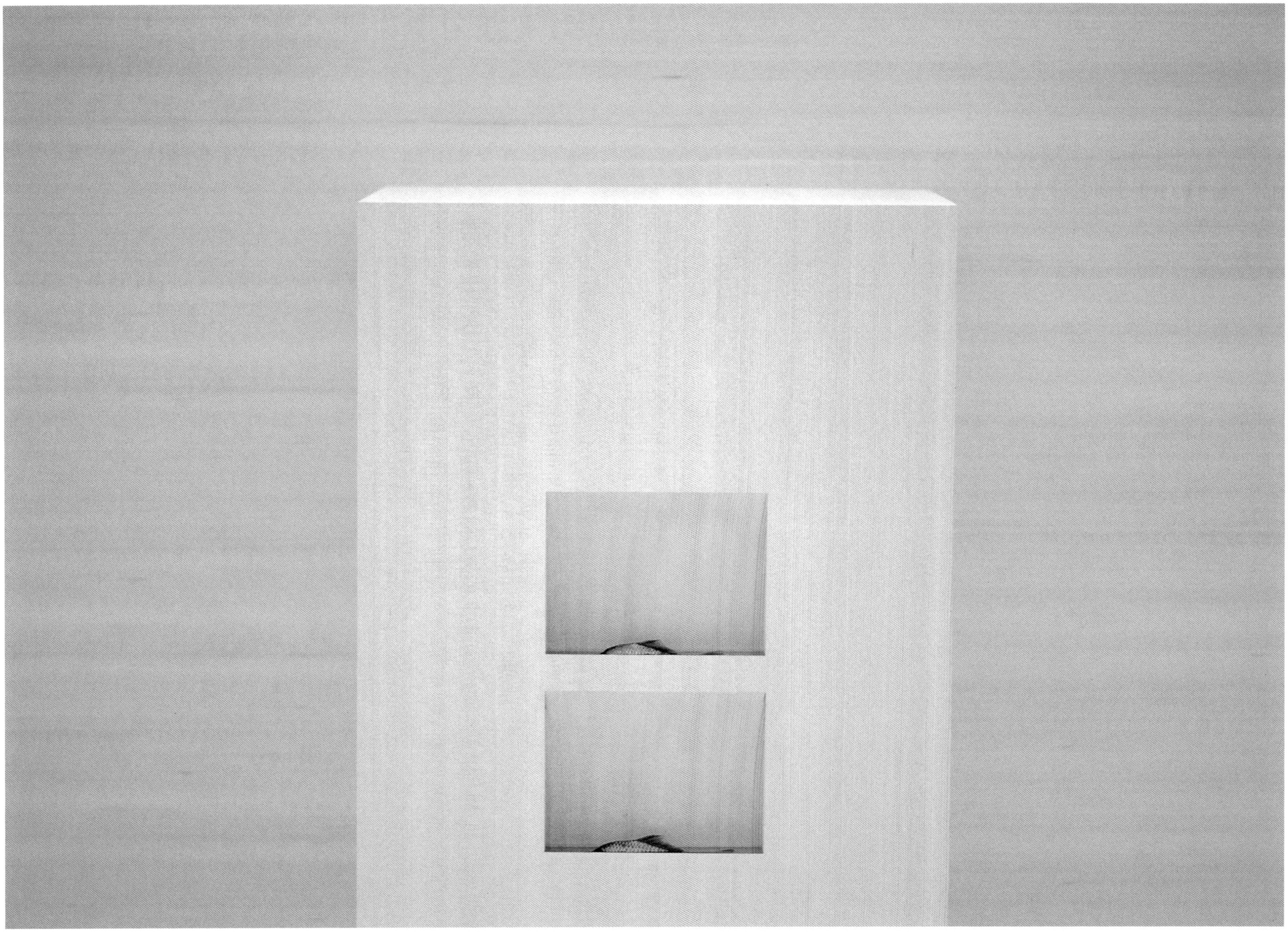

CHIBUKURO (Low cabinet). Plain Wood, Crucian Carps (1456 × 1030)

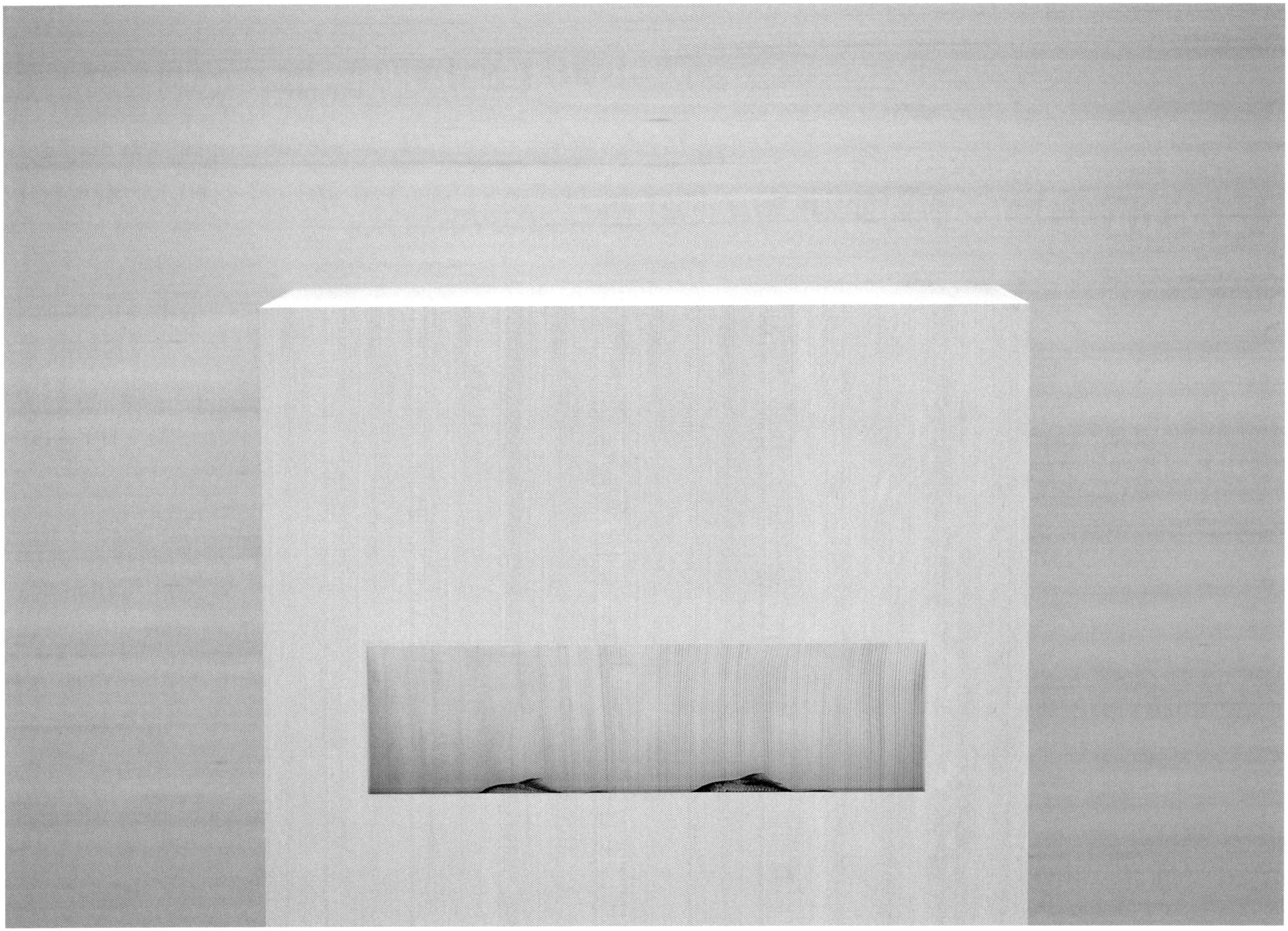

BUDDHIST ALTAR. Plain Wood partly gilded, Crows (1456 × 1030)

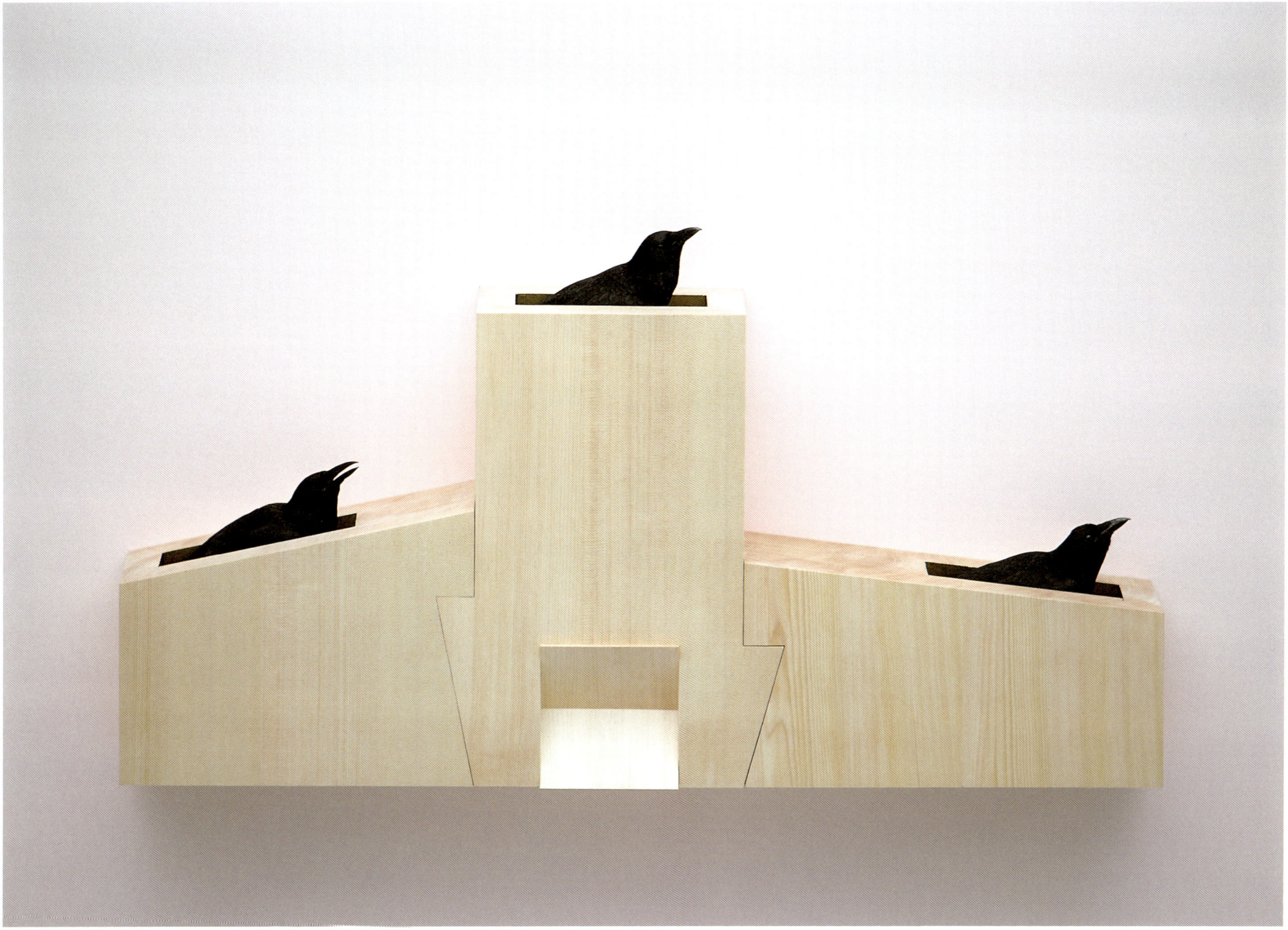

SHELF OF GODS. Plain Wood partly gilded, Crows (1456 × 1030)

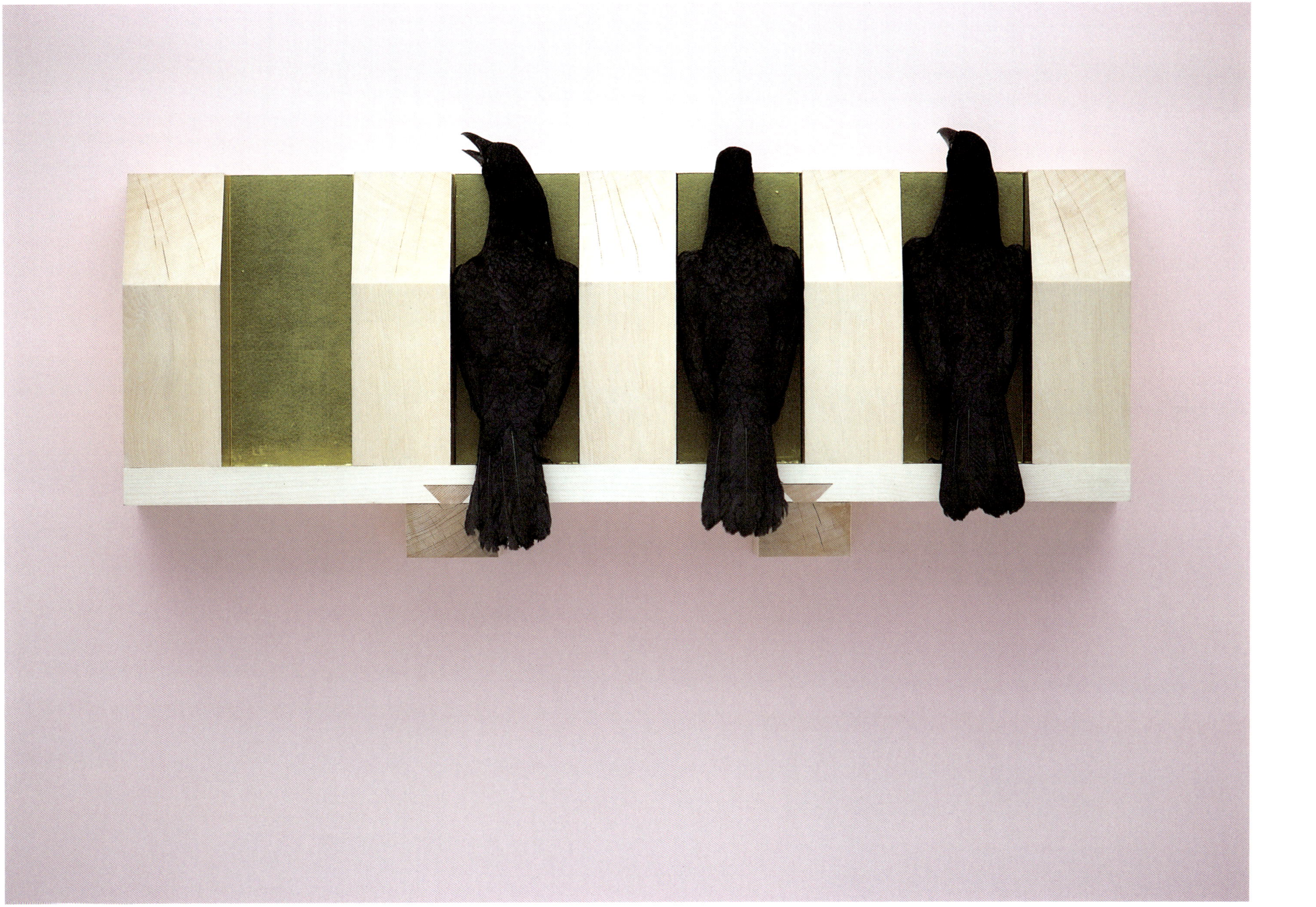

SEIJU TODA: CAREER HISTORY

STUART KLAWANS

Seiju Toda began his artistic career while a student at the public high school in Mikuni, the town in Fukui Prefecture where he had been born in 1948. Through a teacher at the school, Tadahiro Ono—an artist associated with Japan's avant-garde Ande Pada movement—Toda became acquainted with the work of the latest European and American artists. Of these, two in particular—John Cage and Jasper Johns—had a profound impact on the young student.

From Cage, Toda learned that an artwork could be changing and ephemeral—an event happening over time, rather than a static object. From Johns, he learned that the most ordinary things could be made into art, and that artworks could derive their meaning from the way different objects were assembled. Although such ideas were considered novel everywhere in the 1960s, they were especially striking in Japan, where artistic training placed a rigorous emphasis on technical skill.

Most shocking of all, perhaps, was the idea that it might be possible to deny traditional aesthetic values and yet affirm the value of art. "I saw," Toda has said, "that the avant-garde was not just a superficial style but a philosophy."

1965 : Performance Dedicated to John Cage, Mikuni High School.

I first saw the works of Jasper Johns and John Cage when I was in my sophomore year in high school. That was when I decided to pursue a career in art.

My first work, a performance put on at my high school, was dedicated to Cage. I ran two pieces of transparent plastic tubing onto the stage, one coming from the right, the other from the left. Offstage, I stationed volunteers. Their job was to drop marbles into the tubes. The marbles, which were covered in fluorescent paint, glowed as they rolled down the tubes, through a darkened space that was illuminated only by black light. When the marbles got to the center of the stage, they dropped from the ends of the tubes into two receptacles—one a wooden, Japanese-style washtub, the other a Western-style bucket made out of tin. That was my way of addressing the meeting of East and West, of paying tribute to John Cage, and of exploring chance effects of light and sound.

I like to come back to the origin of things. Artists such as Jasper Johns and Pablo Picasso overwhelm viewers with their talent. As for me, I hope to appeal to viewers with my heart.

1966 : *Yomiuri Independent* Exhibition, Sakai City, Osaka.

Each year, the *Yomiuri Independent* newspaper sponsored an exhibition featuring the works of prominent artists such as Shusaku Arakawa, On Kawahara, and Ushio Shinohara. In 1966, while still a high-school student, I found myself selected to exhibit in their company.

How could I make my presence felt among such artists? My answer was to create an installation titled "How to Get to the Place." I ran a piece of transparent plastic tubing through the entire exhibition, at the entrance to which I placed a tank filled with water that had been dyed blue. When visitors arrived, the first thing they saw was the blue water flowing into the tube. They could follow it all the way through the exhibition, past everybody else's work, to the place where the water flowed out—at my site.

The theme of "entrance" and "exit" still intrigues me, since it implies a kind of connection. By running water from a tank to the place where I stood, I created an entrance and an exit. In the same way, if I draw a line in white chalk from my studio to a museum, I am already creating and displaying a work of art. Or I could connect a line from my studio to a river—that, too, would represent "entrance" and "exit."

1967 : "Baby Exhibition"「*Aka-chan Ten*」, Tokiwa Gallery, Tokyo.

My first chance to exhibit at an art gallery came in 1968, when the Tokiwa Gallery invited me to participate in a group show of emerging artists. For my contribution, I covered an entire wall of the gallery with objects made of droplets of transparent synthetic resin. The droplets resembled water. Through the installation, I wanted to express the importance of water to human life.

I also staged a performance at the same time. A bucket filled with water represented the human body. Droplets of water covered the outside of the bucket. That's the nature of water—it can fill things, or it can break down into beads. In my case, I broke the "water" into pieces with a hammer and then put them back into the container.

1968 : "Baby Exhibition," Tokyo.

For the 1968 "Baby Exhibition" at the Tokiwa Gallery, I confronted the theme of, "Which came first, the chicken or the egg?" I stacked 100 chicken coops in the gallery and put a white hen in each. Then, every time an egg was laid, I wrote the date on it and set it aside on display. During the one week of the exhibition, the hens laid 35 eggs. Eventually, of course, there were a lot more, since the installation was presented at various other galleries.

If I had to summarize the installation, I would say that it was trying to express the idea of the genetic code through the image of those neat ranks of hens and carefully dated eggs. Or you could put it another way and say it was about the transmigration of the soul.

1969 : Performance in Front of the Fukui Prefectural Office.

Even the most ordinary routine can come to have a new meaning, if it's done in a novel time and place. For example, you could drink your tea outdoors instead of in a restaurant, or sunbathe in a darkened room, or go through the motions of fishing indoors.

For this performance in front of the Fukui Prefectural Office, I put on a dark cloak, covered my head with bandages, and mimed eating a meal. (The main course, I recall, was soup.) Meanwhile, another performer in an identical costume silently mouthed a poem.

1969 : "Record Exhibition," PARCO Department Store, Tokyo.

In 1960 Jasper Johns made a bronze sculpture of two cans of Ballantine Ale. On one level, it was a negative gesture, since it denied the objects their function. You couldn't drink from Johns's ale cans. On another level, though, the gesture was positive, since it created art. You might say that Johns was "affirming the denial."

Can you take the process a step further? In 1967 I made sculptures out of some records—and the records could actually be played. They contained music by the Beatles and John Cage—and with their surfaces painted in red, blue, yellow, and green oil paint, they were more attractive than the originals.

Perhaps you could turn compact discs into works of art by marking them with the fingerprints of celebrities.

1969 : Three-man Exhibition "Baby Exhibition" 「*Aka-chan Ten*」, Tokiwa Gallery, Tokyo.

1970–73 : One-man Exhibition, Okabe Gallery and PARCO Department Store, Tokyo.

1974 : "The Eye of the Canvas and Light," Muramatsu Gallery, Tokyo.

My work with photography began in 1974 with this installation at Muramatsu Gallery. I mounted canvas panels around the walls of the darkened room. Each panel was printed with a photograph of a beam of light. A real beam of light, of exactly the same sort, was then focused on each panel.

When you closed your eyes and then opened them, the panel looked like either a painted canvas or a piece of sculpture. Either way, the image was created directly by light, which had become an integral part of the artwork.

1974 : One-man Exhibition, Muramatsu Gallery.

1974 : "Image '74 Group Exhibition," Okabe Gallery, Tokyo.

In the same year that I began working with photography, I also made my first exhibition of prints. In part, I was trying to extend my money-making work into the context of art—I had begun a career as a graphic designer. But I also felt that performance art and installation art were played out, at least for me. I had begun to want to make something that would last. The question was, how to make permanent art that would still express my concern with process?

For this exhibition, which also featured the work of Norio Imai and Kenshi, I presented a number of silkscreens titled "Japanese Craftsman's Series." First, I took photographs of objects associated with different crafts—the carpenter's plank, the plasterer's tile. I made rough-grain prints of the photographs, photocopied them, then based the silkscreen prints on the photocopies. The images themselves—the tile or the plank—were abstract and geometric. The methods of reproduction were mechanical. But the texture of the finished print made the viewer highly aware of the process of the art making, while also bringing to mind the handwork of the carpenter or plasterer.

1975 : 100-man Contemporary Block Print Exhibition. Mainichi Contemporary Art Exhibition. Tokyo Invitational Exhibition.

1975–76 : "Image '75 Group Exhibition," Okabe Gallery, Tokyo.

For this show, which included the work of Norio Imai, Masafumi Maita, and Kenshi, I again exhibited silkscreen prints based on photographs. This time, I took photographs of a piece of wood that was in motion, using multiple exposures so as to capture the movement. Then I printed the photographs as silkscreens, using metallic paint and black ink.

To me, movement itself is art. There are four kinds. First is movement in two dimensions, that is, on a plane. Then there is movement in three dimensions. The third type is movement in the imagination. The fourth type is movement with will. All four types may be forms of art.

1976 : One-man Exhibition, Fuma Gallery, Tokyo.

Once again, I made silkscreen prints of photocopies of photographs—this time basing the images on stacks of bricks, which I had wired together and then shattered. To create a second level of the installation, I also made silkscreens based directly on the negatives of the photographs. The *Asahi* newspaper, reviewing the exhibition, compared the work to "a poem . . . told through a naive bright shape, which is the physical metamorphosis of an image of delicate and pure charm."

In 1977 this series was shown at the Azuma Gallery, New York.

1977 : Miami International Block Print Biennial Exhibition. Bradford International Block Print Biennial Exhibition.

One-man Exhibition, Azuma Gallery, New York.

1978 : One-man Exhibition, Fuma Gallery, Tokyo.

In search of an alternative to painting on canvas, I had begun to think about a more direct and physically engaging way of image making: rubbings. You can make a painting of a sofa, say, or a desk, or an automobile. But you can also make a rubbing of the object's surface and get a much different result.

For this series, I prepared a concrete floor by treating it with synthetic resin, glass fiber, and oil colors. Then I drew on the floor geometric designs, bands of color, series of lines, and even images of ordinary objects, such as a bottle. Once I had made the drawings, I transferred those textured designs from the concrete floor onto another surface of synthetic resin. I liked the mixing of the colors, the varied textures, the collagelike effects.

Other works from this series were shown in 1978 at the Okabe Gallery, Tokyo.

1979 : Japan New Face Invitational Exhibition.

1980 : Miami International Block Print Biennial Exhibition.

25th Contemporary Block Print Exhibition, Tokyo Central Gallery.

CWAJ 25th Contemporary Block Print Exhibition, Tokyo American Club.

1981 : One-man Exhibition, Shirota Gallery, Tokyo.

Still searching for new surfaces on which to paint, I tried making a canvas that was not a canvas. Using glass fiber—with a mesh similar to that of coarse canvas—combined with synthetic resin and silicone, I made a molded, textured surface. Then, using oil paints, I added color, creating images that were geometric and abstract but highly textured and expressive in their brushwork.

Someday, I would like to make various "canvases" out of the transferred textures of roads from different countries around the world. I recently tried transferring textures from the ground onto different surfaces, and the results were unbelievably beautiful.

1981 : Hara Annual Invitational Exhibition, Hara Museum, Tokyo.

The chief element in this new surface is Japanese rice paper, *washi*, pasted onto canvas and then treated with silicone, synthetic resin, glass fiber, and oil paint. I wanted above all to emphasize the dry, powdery quality of the *washi*.

I feel that textures are more important than subject matter in my paintings. Sometimes I fantasize about creating a work on a large piece of cloth made from the skins of a whale and an elephant.

1984 : Norway International Block Print Biennial.

Humor in Contemporary Art Exhibition, Museum of Modern Art, Saitama.

One-man Exhibition, Luft Gallery, Tokyo.

1985 : One-man Exhibition, Luft Gallery, Tokyo

Pieces of plain wood are installed inside synthetic resin canvas frames.

Employing linear perspective to create solid objects has already been tried elsewhere; a new challenge was to use the law of perspective to create flat surfaces. This seemingly impossible feat was accomplished first by stripping the drawings off their canvases and then reassembling them into solid forms.

1985 : Photography and Print Project.

This group of photographs and prints represented the four seasons, each symbolized by a different plantlike form made of resin. The resin also resembled crystal. On the "plant" representing summer, I wrote "August 6, 1945" – the day the atomic bomb fell on Hiroshima.

Why did I want to make a "plant" out of crystal – in effect, out of light? I clearly remember the scene in "Close Encounters of the Third Kind" when the UFO, like a giant crystal, comes down to Earth, shining brightly. I thought it was very beautiful. I also remember being in a bar in the Ginza, talking with someone, when I happened to look up and see a chandelier hanging from the ceiling. The bright light of that chandelier is still printed in my mind.

And the brightest light in the world? The first people to look up and see it were in Hiroshima on that day in 1945.

1985 : One-man Exhibition, News Gallery, Tokyo

I spread sand on the floor of the News Gallery and brought in three broken cars. In each of the cars was a video monitor. The image on the screen was the Happy Face character – only it did not remain happy. It would get angry, cry, laugh, then go back to its usual smile.

Human beings and machines alike share "the beauty of breakdown." That was the theme of this installation, which also was a way of crying out for peace. If I had put those Happy Face videos in another setting of breakdown and devastation, for example, an abandoned warehouse, they still would have made the point.

1986–1991 : Projects in X-ray Photography.

In 1986, I began to use X-ray technology as a medium for art photography. The first such piece, which appeared in the newspapers, was of a dead bird with a fishhook in its mouth. How beautiful it was to see light coming through the body of the animal! This wasn't man-made beauty but the natural beauty of life. I realized then that most of what we have seen throughout the long history of art has been a superficial beauty.

For the next five years, I worked on a series of forty pieces, using an industrial X-ray machine as if it were a fine camera. The X-rays revealed the insides of constructions I had built and the insides of living things. They showed things we normally don't see; they combined different layers of objects, which ordinarily we would see successively, into a single image that could be seen all at once. Using the best equipment available and the highest quality of printing, I have strived to refine and improve these works, in the belief that this is truly an art no one has seen before.

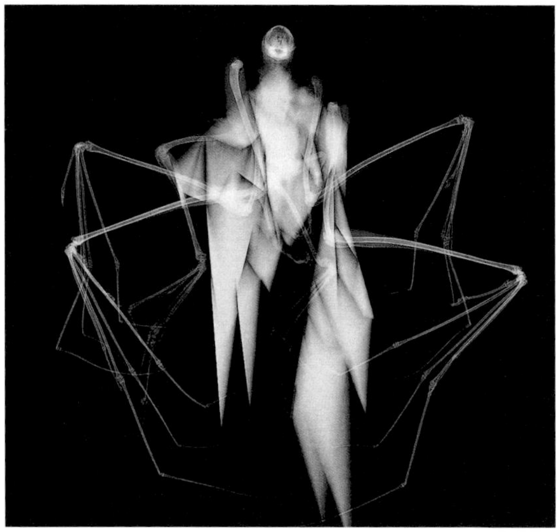

X=t The Bat

1995 : A series composed of the X-ray photographs of the model of "Church of the Light," one of the crowning works of architect Tadao Ando. The model is now part of the permanent collection of MOMA.

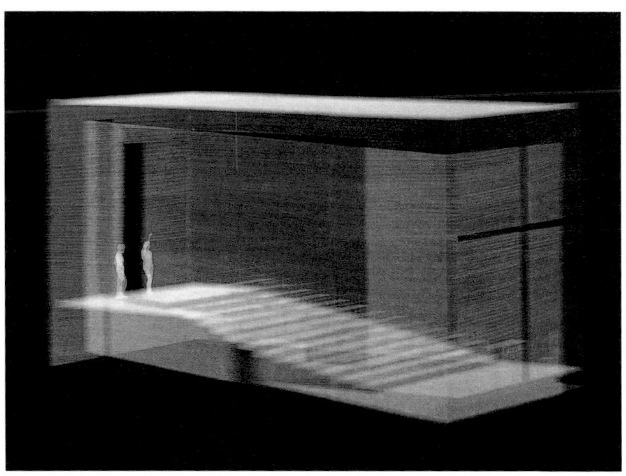

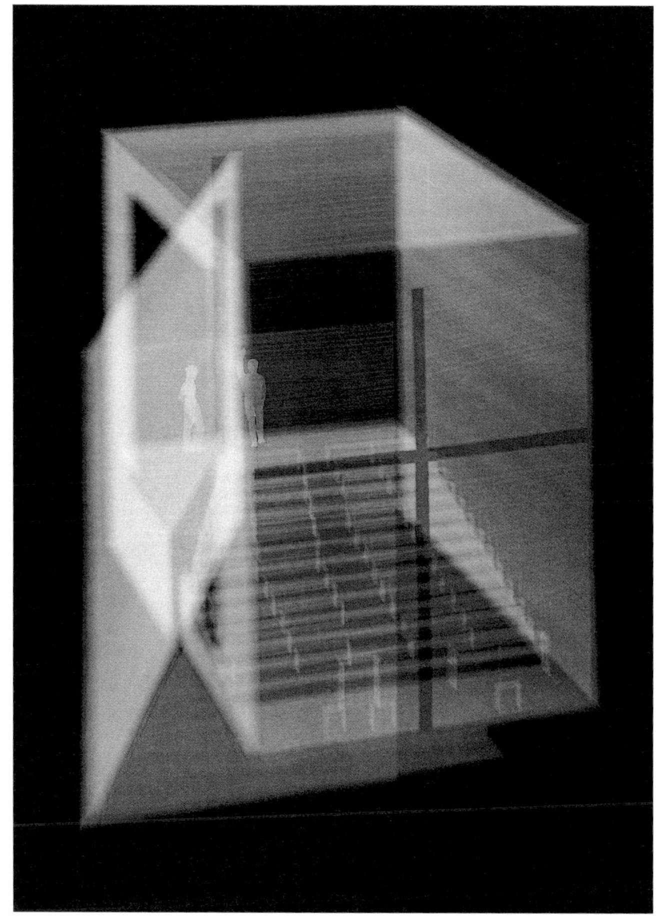

X=t Tadao Ando Church of the light (A model)

1999 : A series that deals with the most universal thing inside us, "soul." And what I expressed visually here is the soul's beauty. To embody the invisible soul, I used the idea of embracing it with skin. By the way, the human body is, in fact, ugly.

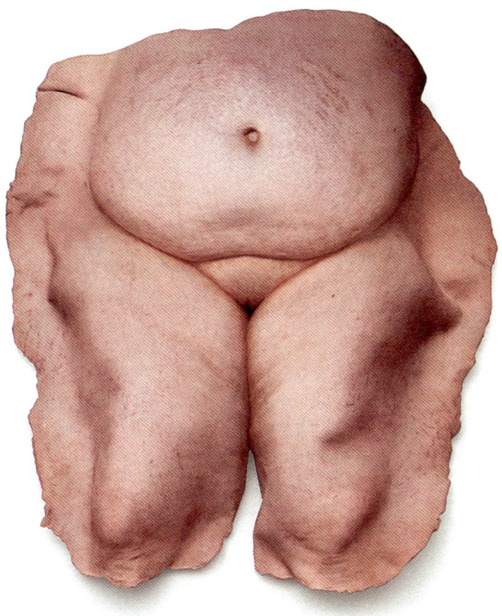

Leather jacket for soul No.1

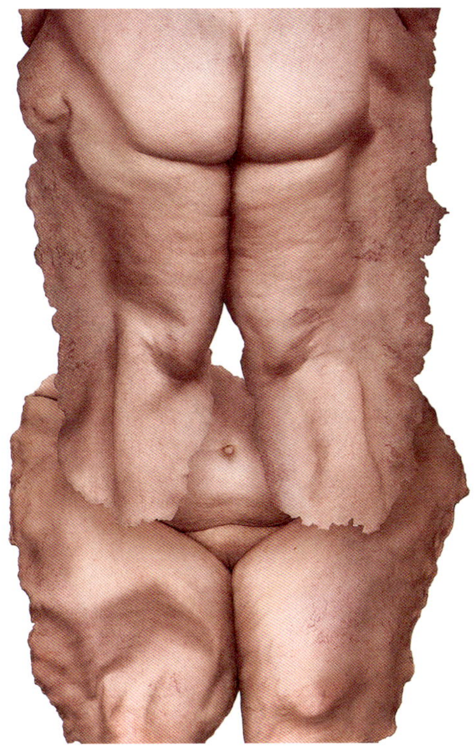

Leather jacket for soul No.2

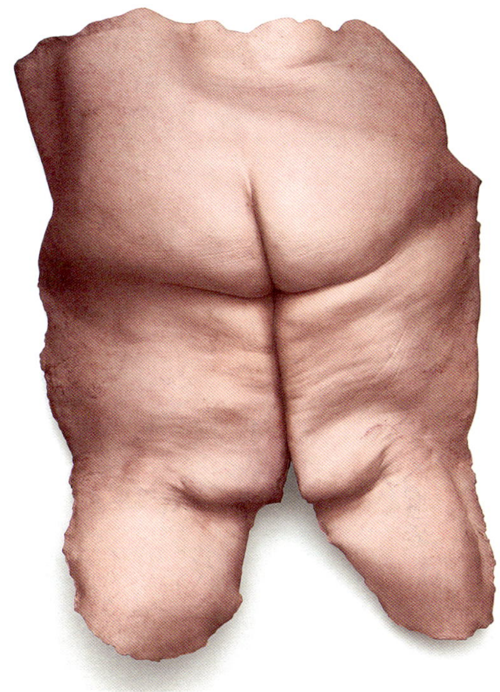

Leather jacket for soul No.3

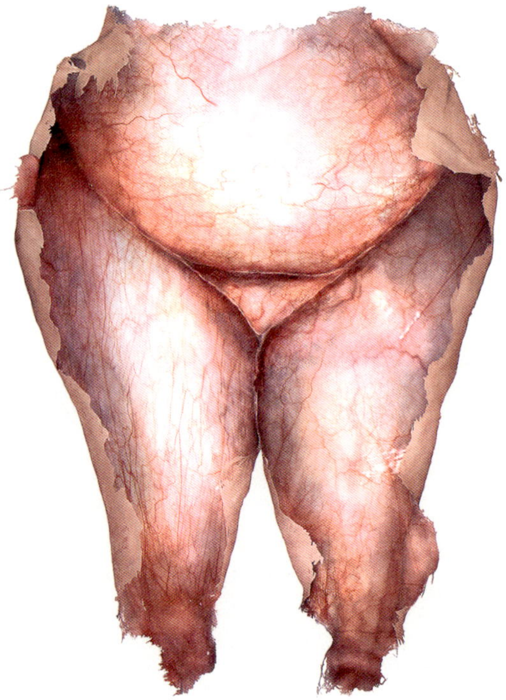

Mother nature

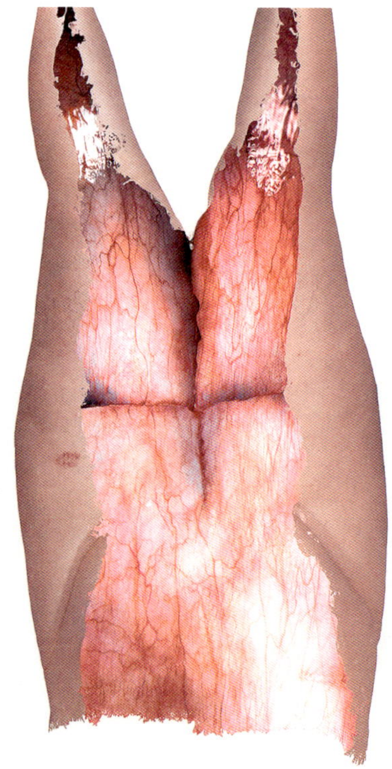

God Bless Human

Selected Major Awards

1983 Grand Prize at International Poster Biennial, Lahti

1984 Museum Prize at Contemporary Japanese Art Exhibition

1985 Excellence Award at the 1st International Anti-War Art Triennial, Rublin

1986 Special Award at 11th International Poster Biennial, Warsaw

1987 Museum Award at 17th International Block Print Biennial, Ljubljana

1989 International Block Print Biennial Museum Award, Cracow

1990 Grand Prix at the International Design Exhibition of France

1993 Grand Prize at Crest International Advertising Award Poster section

1996 Grand Prize at the 17th International Graphic Design Biennial, Brno

1997 Grand Prize at International Poster Biennial, Lahti

2002 Grand Prize at International Graphic Design Biennial, Brno

and many other

Collections

The Chicago Athenaeum

Colorado State University

The Denver Art Museum

Fukui Fine Arts Museum

Lahti Art Museum, Finland

Municipal Museum of Modern Art, Cracow

Municipal Museum of Munich, Germany

Museum fur Kunst und Gewerbe of Mamburg, Germany

The Museum of Modern Art, New York

The Museum of Modern Art, Toyama

National Museum of Modern Art, Ljubljana

National Museum of Oslo, Norway

The University of Connecticut

Warsaw Poster Museum

and many other

Photography

MASAYA SUGA

Staff

TAKU NAKAMURA

MANABU OHASHI

KUMIKO SHINOZUKA

AKINORI KIMURA

JUN MAKI

YOSHINORI MATSUYAMA

NORIKO TAMURA

YOKO YAMAMOTO

Translator

NANAE YAMADA

Printing

Nissha Printing Co., Ltd.